Selfishness, Greed and Capitalism

Selfishness, Greed and Capitalism

Debunking Myths about the Free Market

CHRISTOPHER SNOWDON

The Institute of Economic Affairs

First published in Great Britain in 2015 by
The Institute of Economic Affairs
2 Lord North Street
Westminster
London SW1P 3LB
in association with London Publishing Partnership Ltd
www.londonpublishingpartnership.co.uk

The mission of the Institute of Economic Affairs is to improve understanding
of the fundamental institutions of a free society by analysing and expounding
the role of markets in solving economic and social problems.

A CIP catalogue record for this book is available from the British Library.

ISBN 978-0-255-36677-9

Many IEA publications are translated into languages other
than English or are reprinted. Permission to translate or to reprint
should be sought from the Director General at the address above.

Typeset in Kepler by T&T Productions Ltd
www.tandtproductions.com

Printed and bound in Great Britain by Page Bros

'I think there is a truth, and I think that economists have found a significant amount of the truth in economic behaviour. There are a lot of things we do not know, but there are also a lot of things we do know, which non-economists get completely wrong.'

Gary Becker (Herfeld 2012: 85)

CONTENTS

THE AUTHOR

Christopher Snowdon is the Director of Lifestyle Economics at the IEA. He is the author of *The Art of Suppression*, *The Spirit Level Delusion* and *Velvet Glove, Iron Fist*. He has also authored a number of publications for the IEA, including *Sock Puppets*, *Euro Puppets*, *The Proof of the Pudding*, *The Crack Cocaine of Gambling* and *Free Market Solutions in Health*.

FOREWORD

When the Institute of Economic Affairs was founded, there was particular concern about economic discourse in the class of people F. A. Hayek described as 'intellectuals'. These were people who were widely regarded as speaking with authority but who had no particular capacity for original thinking in relation to many of the issues on which they commented. One good example of such a person would be a member of the clergy when speaking about economic issues. It is true that he may have expertise in relation to some aspects of the subject, such as how to determine what is and what is not ethical behaviour in business. However, on technical aspects of economics and public finance, clergy probably know no more than the average layperson.

In recent years, a number of popular books on economics have come to the fore which are widely read and quoted by exactly the kinds of people Hayek identified. Some, such as those by Naomi Klein, are written by non-economists: in other words by the same intellectual class which is the source of the problem Hayek was identifying. Others are written by people with a strong academic record, such as Ha-Joon Chang. Chang comes in for some criticism in this monograph but it cannot be argued that he is a mere second-hand dealer in ideas.

In some of these popular economics texts, ideas that are arguable are sometimes presented as fact (or at least without consideration of contrary evidence) and certain things are said that are the complete reverse of the truth. A particularly favoured tactic of such authors is to argue that supporters of a market economy believe in certain things which they do not believe in at all (that is, a 'straw man' is erected). The straw man is then demolished and the reader is led to believe that the case for the market economy falls with it.

The misuse of economics is not confined to discussion of policy issues in the public square. Economics now feeds in to many subjects taught in schools and universities. In schools, subjects such as geography, and even science and religious education, involve the presentation of economic principles. In many degrees at universities (for example, business studies, international relations and geography) modules cover economic principles.

When economic ideas are taught in these contexts, there is not necessarily the proper analysis and discussion which would be expected in a specialist course. Teaching materials are provided to generalists and they tend to present 'facts' or 'principles' that are assumed to not need discussion and which are highly debatable.

This monograph is a very effective attempt to correct economic myths that prevail in public discourse and which are often promoted in schools and even universities. It begins by examining straw men, such as the assertion that economists believe that people behave selfishly or that economists think that GDP is all that matters. The fact that economists do not believe these things at all is easily established and it is surprising that eminent economists with good publication records (albeit not in the philosophy of economics) can honestly argue otherwise.

The author, Christopher Snowdon, then moves on to look at myths that can be subjected to empirical analysis and easily shown to be false. These myths, such as the idea that the poor are getting poorer while the rich get richer, or that we are working longer hours, are easily rebutted.

Christopher Snowdon performs a very important service in this book, which is a significant contribution to the Institute's educational mission. The chapters are all very easy to read and rich with the necessary evidence. Anybody interested in economics or who is studying economics will find the points the author makes important in their own right. It will be even more valuable for those who have previously been introduced to the myths that are rebutted. The myths the author deals with are very widespread as they have been taken on board and regularly repeated by newspaper columnists, others in the media and economic commentators more generally.

PHILIP BOOTH
Editorial and Programme Director
Institute of Economic Affairs
Professor of Insurance and Risk Management
Cass Business School, City University, London
October 2014

The views expressed in this monograph are, as in all IEA publications, those of the author and not those of the Institute (which has no corporate view), its managing trustees, Academic Advisory Council members or senior staff. With some exceptions, such as with the publication of lectures, all IEA monographs are blind peer-reviewed by at least two academics or researchers who are experts in the field.

PREFACE

This book is divided into two sections. The first four chapters deal with 'straw man' assertions that are sometimes made about free-market economics. For critics of the market economy, it is easier to respond to absurd distortions of their opponents' position than to tackle their arguments directly. The most common exaggerations and misrepresentations about economists' beliefs and assumptions are dealt with in Part 1.

Part 2 addresses specific claims that can be shown to be false. These claims typically portray the state of economic life in the twenty-first century in a gloomier light than can be justified by empirical evidence. Pervasive beliefs about Britons working longer and longer hours for less and less pay are addressed in this section, along with claims about inequality, social mobility and happiness.

If this book makes the reader more interested in the role of free markets in improving society, then so much the better, but that is not its main intention. Its intention is to help those interested in and who comment on economic matters to distinguish between fact and fiction in areas where facts can be clearly proven and myths debunked. This is not a book about economic theory, nor does it attempt to settle major controversies. On the few occasions where the subject matter touches on a genuine academic debate, this is acknowledged in the text. For the most part, however, the questions posed can be answered by consulting evidence that is widely available or – in the case of the straw men – listening to what economists actually say.

This book is dedicated to *The Guardian* newspaper, a constant source of inspiration.

SUMMARY

- It is often asserted that supporters of a market
  economy believe that 'greed is good'. This is simply not
  true. Economists know that people are capable of a
  range of thoughts, feelings, motivations and emotions
  and a market economy works regardless of whether
  people are selfish or altruistic.
- A further straw man often erected by opponents of
  market economies is that free-market economists
  assume that individuals always behave with perfect
  rationality. Again, this is not true, though it is assumed
  that individuals are better placed to know their own
  preferences than government planners or officials.
- It is frequently suggested that the rich are getting
  richer while the poor get poorer. For example: '[the]
  late 70s saw the most equal time in British history, but
  since then the rich have got richer and the poor poorer'
  (Polly Toynbee writing in 2012). This is false. Between
  1977 and 2011/12, the incomes of the poorest fifth of
  the population have risen by 93 per cent. It is also not
  true that median earnings have stagnated. Median
  earners saw their hourly wage rise by 62 per cent
  between 1986 and 2011.
- The average number of hours worked by British
  workers continues to fall. It fell from 37.7 hours a

week in 2000 to 36.4 per week in 2011, having fallen from 38.1 hours in 1992. Fewer than 12 per cent of British employees work more than fifty hours a week. Working hours in Britain are neither much longer nor much shorter than those in other wealthy countries.

- The reason we have not reduced our working hours to the extent that Keynes, for example, believed likely is that we aspire to a lifestyle that is better than a typical 1930s working class lifestyle without central heating, hot running water, a telephone, wall-to-wall carpets, a car, an indoor toilet, a computer, a television and so on.

- Many commentators argue that the UK is suffering from growing inequality. For example, Deborah Hargreaves, director of The High Pay Centre, asserts that 'Inequality has been rising rapidly in Britain for the past 30 years ... If the growth in inequality continues at its current rate, we are heading towards Victorian extremes in the next 20 years.' Such statements are not true. The peak in inequality was in 1990 and the income gap has been flat or in decline ever since. Between 1990 and 2006–7, those in the bottom quintile increased their disposable income by 40 per cent, a faster rate than was seen among the top quintile, whose disposable income rose by only 29 per cent. In 2011–12, income inequality in Britain fell to its lowest level since 1986. It is only within the top 10 per cent of income earners that incomes are becoming more unequal.

- Once income has been redistributed through tax, cash payments and benefits in kind, the ratio between the incomes of the top and bottom fifth of the population is reduced from 14 to 1 to 4 to 1. This is almost exactly the same ratio as in 1987.

- Many claims have been made about the relationship between inequality and various social outcomes such as murder rates, health outcomes and so on, especially in *The Spirit Level*. However, the claims do not stand up to thorough scrutiny. They are often reliant on outliers within the data or the particular way in which the relevant countries were selected. These issues have been studied much more thoroughly by specialists who come to more nuanced conclusions about how social outcomes can be improved.

- The authors of *The Spirit Level* argue that there is a relationship between reduced inequality and happiness. However, there is a stronger relationship between happiness and higher average incomes. While there is good reason to be sceptical about 'happiness economics' it would seem just from these figures that the best strategy to increase happiness would be to reduce poverty through faster national income growth – even if this led to higher inequality.

- It is not true that social mobility has ground to a halt, nor is Alan Milburn correct when he says that 'we still live in a country where, invariably, if you're born poor, you die poor'. Over the last generation, if the income of a boy's parents was in the poorest quarter of the income distribution, the probability of the boy moving into the top half of the income distribution is 37 per cent. If the income of a boy's parents was in the top quarter of the income distribution, the probability of the boy moving into the bottom half of the income distribution is 33 per cent. There is substantial mobility within society.

FIGURES AND TABLES

PART 1

THE STRAW MEN

1 CAPITALISM RELIES ON GREED AND SELFISHNESS

In his best-selling book *23 Things They Don't Tell You About Capitalism*, Ha-Joon Chang says that free-market economists regard people as 'tunnel-visioned self-seeking robots', 'totally selfish' and 'selfish, amoral agents' (Chang 2010: 46, 47, 50). 'Free-market ideology,' he claims, 'is built on the belief that people won't do anything "good" unless they are paid for it or punished for not doing it' (255). Richard Murphy, who bills himself as the UK's number one economics blogger, claims that economists assume people to be entirely self-interested and that their self-interest manifests itself in the desire for ever-greater consumption of material goods. He says that economics, as taught in schools and universities, is 'predicated on the belief that human beings' behaviour is solely focused on maximising their own individual returns; that businesses maximise their profit and that everything that indicates success in life depends on consuming more' (Murphy 2011: 12).

If this is a fair representation of what economics is all about, economics is obviously flawed. We can all readily think of acts of altruism which contradict the theory of total selfishness, and none of us feel that we are wholly driven by consumerism. If free-market economics is based on the belief that everybody is relentlessly greedy all the time, it is not just simplistic but wrong. Chang (2010: 255) writes:

> People are *not* as much propelled by material self-interest as free-market textbooks claim. If the real world were as full of rational self-seeking agents as the one depicted in those textbooks, it would collapse under the weight of continuous cheating, monitoring, punishment and bargaining.

The task of debunking free-market economics is therefore an easy one. If economists believe that everybody is selfish and greedy all the time, it only requires a few examples of selflessness and altruism to undermine the entire field. The problem is that they do *not* believe that.

Incentives and the invisible hand

The straw man claim made by critics of the free market comes in two parts. Firstly, that economists believe that everybody is utterly selfish and, secondly, that capitalism *requires* people to be utterly selfish.

On the first point, Chang argues that 'Free market economics starts from the assumption that all economic agents are selfish, as summed up in Adam Smith's assessment of the butcher, the brewer and the baker' (Chang 2010: 43). This is a reference to the famous line in Adam Smith's *The Wealth of Nations* (1776): 'It is not from the benevolence of the butcher, the brewer, or the baker that we expect our dinner, but from their regard of their own interest' (Smith 1957: 13).[1] It is questionable whether someone who does not want to work for free is 'selfish', as Chang puts it, and it is puzzling why Smith's obvious truism should invite scorn. It is surely self-evident that butchers, brewers and bakers do not supply us with their products out of the goodness of their hearts. '[M]an has almost constant occasion for the help of others,' wrote Smith, but 'it is vain for him to expect it from their benevolence only' (Smith 1957: 13).

In normal economic transactions, we expect each party to seek an outcome that benefits them, but this does not imply that people are entirely self-interested when they are not making economic transactions (such as spending time with friends and family), nor does it imply that altruistic behaviour such as giving to charity is abnormal. Like Chang, many critics of capitalism use 'self-interest' and 'selfishness' (or 'greed') interchangeably, but they are quite different. Selfishness implies indulging oneself at another's expense, but free-market transactions only take place when two self-interested parties see a mutual benefit.

Self-interest should not be conflated with avarice. If I decide to have apple juice instead of orange juice with my breakfast I am acting in my self-interest, but unless I snatch it from a thirsty child I can hardly be accused of

---

1 Like many classic texts, Smith's book is more talked about than read. Those who do not have time to read it all should at least read its full title: *An Inquiry into the Nature and Causes of the Wealth of Nations*. Unlike so many critics of capitalism, Smith understood that it is wealth that has 'causes', not poverty.

selfishness. Neither is taking a holiday or an education course generally selfish, but these things may still be a legitimate pursuit of self-interest. The desire to fulfil wants and needs in no way implies greed. Adam Smith wrote of the 'uniform, constant, and uninterrupted effort of every man to better his condition' (Smith 1957: 306). Self-interest can mean wanting to provide a better life for ourselves and our families, but it can encompass altruism and a host of non-financial ambitions.

Many argue that self-interest should not be seen in purely economic terms, but, instead, as a broader term to describe our goals and aspirations. Milton and Rose Friedman, for example, wrote (Friedman and Friedman 1980: 27):

> Narrow preoccupation with the economic market has led to a narrow interpretation of self-interest as myopic selfishness, as exclusive concern with immediate material rewards. Economics has been berated for allegedly drawing far-reaching conclusions from a wholly unrealistic 'economic man' who is little more than a calculating machine, responding only to monetary stimuli. That is a great mistake. Self-interest is not myopic selfishness. It is whatever it is that interests the participants, whatever they value, whatever goals they pursue. The scientist seeking to advance the frontiers of his discipline, the missionary seeking to convert infidels to the true faith, the philanthropist seeking to bring comfort to the needy – all are pursuing their interests, as they see them, as they judge them by their own values.

Adam Smith never suggested that financial self-interest is, or ought to be, our sole motivation in life. He taught philosophy at the University of Edinburgh and wrote at length about ethics and altruism. In his earlier book *The Theory of Moral Sentiments*,[2] Smith expanded on his view that humans were profoundly driven by empathy for their fellow man (Smith 1759: 1):

> How selfish soever man may be supposed, there are evidently some principles in his nature, which interest him in the fortune of others, and render their happiness necessary to him, though he derives nothing from it, except the pleasure of seeing it.

Anyone familiar with Smith's life and work knows that he was by no means entirely driven by financial self-interest, nor did he assume that anybody else was. He was acutely aware that there was more to life than material possessions and he wrote a whole book about it, but *The Wealth of Nations* is not that book. *The Wealth of Nations* is about economics, and financial self-interest cannot be ignored in a book about economics. The fundamental aim of any business is to turn a profit. The butcher might occasionally give a day's takings to charity and the baker may

2 Since *The Wealth of Nations* was published seventeen years after *The Theory of Moral Sentiments*, some have suggested that Smith abandoned his belief in mankind's benevolence in favour of a model of cold self-interest in the interim. In fact, large sections of the later book were taken verbatim from lectures he gave fifteen years earlier so this is most unlikely (see Butler 2007: 15).

sometimes offer a loaf for free, but altruism of this sort cannot be the core activity of a business and they are not assumptions upon which a sound economic theory can be based.

The crucial point is that in a free market it makes no difference whether the entrepreneur is impeccably well-intentioned or unashamedly self-serving. Introducing the famous phrase 'the invisible hand', Smith (1957: 400) wrote:

> by directing that industry in such a manner as its produce may be of the greatest value, he intends only his own gain, and he is in this, as in many other cases, led by an invisible hand to promote an end which was no part of his intention.

Here are two of Smith's key lessons. Firstly, that each person can best pursue their own interests by serving the interests of others – there is no need for force or central planning. By pursuing 'his own gain', the individual adds value to the economy and benefits his fellow man. The benefits extend to people he has never met and whose company he may not enjoy. The self-interest of the butcher and the brewer makes life easier for those who do not want to slaughter their own livestock and make their own beer. The butcher does not have to go to the trouble of baking his own bread, and the baker can use the profit he makes to buy from the brewer. The profit motive ensures a supply of bread, meat and beer at a lower cost and of a better quality than each worker could provide for himself.

The second lesson is that these mutual benefits come about despite the individual being an unwitting and unconscious player. The profit motive provides incentives for people to do good even when they are not trying to. A selfish and uncharitable entrepreneur can benefit society by meeting the wants and needs of his customers. Indeed, he will *have* to meet their wants and needs if he is to prosper in business. He may understand the laws of economics or may be totally ignorant, but so long as he labours for himself, he 'necessarily labours to render the annual revenue of the society as great as he can' even though he 'neither intends to promote the public interest, nor knows how much he is promoting it.'

Smith's great heresy was to show that there is nothing grubby or disreputable about selling at a profit. Friedrich Hayek believed that Smith's ideas 'offended a deeply ingrained instinct that man ... should aim at doing a visible good to his known fellows (the "neighbour" of the Bible). These are the feelings that still, under the name of "social justice", govern all socialist demands and easily engage the sympathies of all good men, but which are irreconcilable with the open society to which today all the inhabitants of the West owe the general level of their wealth' (Hayek 1991: 118). Today, even those critics who concede that capitalism successfully creates growth and prosperity retain their disgust at the mechanism of self-interest that drives it. Skidelsky and Skidelsky (2012: 5), for example, complain that 'the present system relies on motives of greed and acquisitiveness, which are morally repugnant.'

Many people find it incongruous that noble ends can result from ignoble – or at least morally neutral – motives. 'The public has severe doubts about how much it can count on profit-seeking business to produce socially beneficial outcomes,' writes Bryan Caplan. 'They focus on the *motives* of business, and neglect the discipline imposed by competition' (Caplan 2007: 30; emphasis in the original). The observation that man can help others by helping himself is easily mistaken for a celebration of greed and selfishness. And since greed is morally objectionable, nothing good should come of it – the best intentions should result in the best outcomes. But Smith showed this to be untrue. Not only did those who worked for profit often do good for society, but those who professed to be working for society often did ill. 'I have never known much good done by those who affected to trade for the public good,' he wrote (Smith 1957: 400). The reasons for this are discussed in the next chapter.

In short, the pursuit of self-interest is not the same as greed. The brewer, the baker and the butcher may not be providing beer, meat and bread motivated by the needs of others. However, there is nothing grubby, ignoble or even necessarily greedy about pursuing a business or career to provide for one's family. Some supporters of a free market may celebrate greed; others may see greed as self-interest gone too far. It is benign self-interest which believers in a free market regard as the motives for economic action and not greed and selfishness. However, supporters of a free market would also argue that greed in the context of a market economy causes much less harm than greed exercised by those who have political control over the allocation of resources.

The parable of the steel company

In applied cost–benefit analyses economists typically assume a large element of narrow self-interest. There is no compelling evidence to suggest that they are mistaken. The matter-of-fact observation that butchers and bakers work for money does not preclude them from enjoying their work, nor does it preclude them from working for nothing if they can afford to. It merely reminds us that without financial incentives very little work would get done.

Why, then, does Chang think that his fellow economists are wrong in believing that people's financial decisions are largely driven by self-interest? A clue to his thinking comes when he quotes the manager of the Japanese company, Kobe Steel, whom he once heard speak at a conference. This gentleman stood up in front of a panel of economists and, as Chang recalls, delivered the following speech (Chang 2010: 43):

> I am sorry to say this, but you economists don't understand how the real world works. I have a PhD in metallurgy and have been working in Kobe Steel for nearly three decades, so I know a thing or two about steel-making. However, my company is now so large and complex that even I do not understand more than half the things that are going on within it. As for the other managers – with backgrounds in accounting and marketing – they

> really don't have much of a clue. Despite this, our board of directors routinely approves the majority of projects submitted by our employees, because we believe that our employees work for the good of the company. If we assumed that everyone is out to promote their own interests and questioned the motivations of our employees all the time, the company would grind to a halt, as we would spend all our time going through proposals that we really don't understand. You simply cannot run a large bureaucratic organisation, be it Kobe Steel or your government, if you assume that everyone is out for himself.

Chang describes this little monologue as 'a powerful testimony to the limitations of standard economic theory, which assumes that self-interest is the only human motivation that counts.' But let us look at what this manager is actually saying. He is describing a business that has become too large for any single individual to be able to supervise every aspect of its operation. Naturally, therefore, a certain amount of trust has to be placed in the staff. It is possible that this trust could be misplaced and that middle managers are putting forward foolish proposals that will lose the company money. It is also possible that the staff could abuse this trust by stealing from the company.

Since neither of these undesirable outcomes appears to have resulted, the manager believes that his staff are not as self-serving as an economist would assume. But he is wrong. In truth, the employees are being guided by the same incentives and disincentives as Adam Smith's victuallers. Unless Kobe Steel is a very peculiar firm, its workers will not be volunteers but salaried employees who have been recruited on the basis of qualifications, references and interview. If it is like most companies, it will award bonuses to employees who advance its corporate interests. It almost certainly incentivises staff with promotions and pay rises. Less productive staff may be denied promotion or even face the sack. It is precisely *because* the workers are incentivised to promote the interests of the company that its senior managers do not have to question their motives and can trust their proposals. By aligning the interests of shareholders, directors, management and staff, Kobe Steel harnesses self-interest to create prosperity and harmony. As Taleb (2007: 17) says, 'the great strength of the free-market system is the fact that company executives don't need to know what's going on.' There is no conflict between working for the good of the company and promoting one's own interest. This is not a testimony to the limits of standard economics. It is the invisible hand in action.[3]

The manager quoted above takes the view – which Chang appears to share – that an employee's self-interest can best be advanced by embezzling, stealing and cheating. Remember that Chang thinks that classical economists view people as 'selfish, amoral agents' and should therefore be happy to engage in criminal behaviour. Since

---

3 It is worth noting that, even if the employees are only motivated by making good steel and not by the desire for maintaining or advancing their position in the company, this is still part of what determines their self-interest. Intellectual curiosity, the desire to do a good job and the satisfaction of making something can all motivate people.

the employees of Kobe Steel are apparently honest, Chang feels vindicated in his view that the economists are wrong.

But surely the company has disincentives as well as incentives? Even if the character of the staff at Kobe Steel is beyond reproach, it would be surprising if the company does not have regulations and a disciplinary process which will occasionally result in dismissals. It may also have some form of video surveillance system on its premises. Businesses have regulations, surveillance and disciplinary procedures not because they assume that everybody is a greedy crook but because a few people are.[4] We have laws against murder and theft for the same reason – to deal with a minority of criminals, not because we assume that everybody is a 'selfish, amoral agent'.

Safeguards against misconduct in the workplace are perfectly consistent with the free-market view that economic life be regulated to prevent corruption, extortion and theft. For most employees, the benefits they receive from working hard, combined with the threat of

---

4   As it happens, not every person who has worked at Kobe Steel is impeccably well behaved. In 2006, an investigation revealed that 'data on soot and smoke released by one of its plants were falsified frequently over a period of 30 years' (*Japan Times*, 2006). In 2009, the chairman resigned over 'inappropriate donations' given to politicians. In 2002, six former Kobe Steel executives and a corporate racketeer agreed to pay 310 million yen to the company after a payoff scandal. In the latter case, the judge remarked: 'Top executives of a company cannot avoid responsibility by simply making the excuse that they did not know (about the wrongdoings of their subordinates)' (*Japan Times*, 2002).

dismissal or prosecution if they shirk or steal, means that their self-interest is best advanced by furthering the interests of the company. The carrot may be a greater incentive than the stick, but neither relies on the employee's benevolence. The manager of Kobe Steel assumes that employees who are 'out to promote their own interests' cannot also 'work for the good of the company'. In fact, the framework of incentives provided by the employer means that the two objectives are perfectly compatible.

Is greed good?

Is there a sense in which 'greed is good'? Adam Smith would never have used such a crass phrase, not least because he did not believe it. Those words were spoken by the fictional Gordon Gekko, an executive at the fictional company Teldar Paper, and were written by the left-wing film director Oliver Stone in the 1987 corporate satire *Wall Street*. Even this grotesque caricature of a wheeler-dealer admits that the word 'greed' is not wholly satisfactory as a description of the mechanism that drives economic progress:

> Greed, for lack of a better word, is good. Greed is right. Greed works. Greed clarifies, cuts through, and captures the essence of the evolutionary spirit. Greed, in all of its forms; greed for life, for money, for love, knowledge, has marked the upward surge of mankind and greed, you mark my words, will not only save Teldar Paper, but that other malfunctioning corporation called the U.S.A.

In the film, greed turns out to be not so good for Gordon Gekko, who is convicted of insider trading and sent to prison. Free-market economists would have shed no tears for the man. They know that greed can lead to great evils and that markets must be circumscribed within the rule of law. Greed is *not* good. It can lead us towards criminality, as it did with the fictional Gordon Gekko and the real-life Bernie Madoff; but theft, deceit and corruption are risks in any society. For good or ill, selfishness and avarice – and, for that matter, sloth and lust – are also features of any society, be it feudal, socialist or capitalist. They are not unique to free markets and there is no reason to believe that capitalism breeds them. To quote Tom Palmer (2011: 66):

> I know of no good reason to think that markets promote selfishness or greed, in the sense that market interaction increases the quantum of greediness or the propensity of people to be selfish, over what is observed in societies governed by states that suppress or discourage or interfere in or disrupt markets.

But while greed is not good, it is senseless to pretend that it does not exist or that it can somehow be erased from the character of mankind. Whereas self-interest can only be pursued in tribal, feudal or socialist societies at the expense of others through the pursuit of power, free-market capitalism is able to harness self-interest and direct it towards activities that are beneficial to others. As David Boaz (2011: 35) puts it:

Critics of markets often complain that capitalism encourages and rewards self-interest. In fact, people are self-interested under any political system. Markets channel their self-interest in socially beneficent directions. In a free market, people achieve their own purposes by finding out what others want and trying to offer it.

Capitalism does not *rely* on selfish motives, but it is able to put selfish motives to good ends where such motives exist. In any case, the moral objection that capitalism 'rewards greed' (Kaufman 2012: xi) is ill-founded. Greedy men dislike free markets because the existence of competition prevents them from charging too much and providing too little. They are forever seeking special protection from the government to make markets less free, keep prices high and exclude competitors. Capitalism is robust against selfishness, not dependent on it. Socialism, by contrast, depends on altruism. In the words of Arthur Seldon (2004: 344):

The virtue of capitalism is that it divorces purpose from result. It does not require good men or women. The vice of socialism is that men and women who may start with good intentions, but who are skilled in acquiring coercive power, can use it to do harm.

Ha-Joon Chang claims that an economic system that relied on 'the self-seeking individuals found in economic textbooks ... would grind to a halt because we would be spending most of our time cheating, trying to catch the cheaters, and punishing the caught' (Chang 2010: 41). Such a society would, he says 'collapse under the weight of continuous cheating, monitoring, punishment and bargaining' (Chang 2010: 255). In fact, this is a pretty good description of what happened in the socialist utopias of Eastern Europe in the twentieth century. Continual monitoring and punishment were necessary in those unfortunate countries precisely because there was no invisible hand to peacefully direct labour towards socially beneficial outcomes. By replacing the invisible hand of free enterprise with the dead hand of the state, communist societies were forced to rely on surveillance and propaganda to keep workers in line. Without adequate financial incentives to reward them, citizens felt little urge to toil for the betterment of society. Their self-interest was best served by shirking, cheating and stealing. As the Russian joke went: 'We pretend to work and they pretend to pay us.'

Conclusion

Economists do not assume that greed is good, nor do they assume that people are wholly selfish. Like everybody else, they know that people are capable of a range of thoughts, feelings, motivations and emotions. The important point is that the free market works regardless of whether people are selfish or altruistic. But if one rejects self-interest as the key motivation that drives the economy, it is a short step to concluding that people do things because ... well, because *they just do*. Without the profit motive as an explanation, we have to imagine that those who work hard do so because they enjoy working, not because of the surplus income they earn. And if people do not respond to financial incentives in a rational or predictable way, there can be little disincentive effect from raising taxes. Hence Richard Murphy can assert that 'entrepreneurial activity is a lifestyle choice that genuine entrepreneurs take irrespective of taxes' (Murphy 2011: 283) while Joseph Stiglitz can endorse any income tax level up to and including 100 per cent, saying 'I can agree with Laffer[5] that if you tax people at 100 per cent they might not work, but even then you have plenty of people who are not motivated by money' (Smith 2012).

Chang's message – and the title of the chapter in which he takes on Adam Smith – is 'assume the worst about people and you get the worst', but this is an empty cliché. Assumptions have little impact on how people behave, it is how you treat them that counts. The irony is that Chang does *not* assume the best about people. Like many left-wingers, he emphasises mankind's benevolent and compassionate nature while supporting policies which suggest that society will descend into chaos and degradation unless the government regulates almost every conceivable activity and transaction. He does not expect to get the best out of bankers and chief executives by assuming the best about them. Instead he supports bans on various financial services and limits on executive pay. Chang does not recommend that the government step aside and allow people's 'non-selfish

---

5   Arthur Laffer is best known for the 'Laffer Curve', which shows that tax revenues decline when tax rates are set too high.

behaviours' and 'moral codes' to flourish (Chang 2010: 50). On the contrary, he concludes that 'government needs to become bigger and more active' (260).

Supporters of a free market, on the other hand, are caricatured as having a bleak view of mankind while espousing policies that emphasise voluntary co-operation with minimal restraints on human behaviour. This circle can only be squared if we understand that they do not, in fact, believe that people are heartless, self-serving agents. The only group of intellectuals who consistently claim that we are self-serving, consumerism-obsessed materialists are left-wing thinkers such as Oliver James, who rails against 'selfish capitalists'. As Kenneth Minogue (1989: 23–24) observed, it is the egalitarian who believes that 'most people are selfish and greedy, but that governments can act morally on their behalf'.

Simply put, economists assume that people are largely driven by self-interest when it comes to financial transactions. This is not an article of faith, rather it is an observation based on the revealed preferences of real people in every society since time immemorial. As Binmore (2007: 4–5) notes, empirical research

> only supports the conclusion that for most adequately incentified people in most economic environments in developed societies, the data can be explained without assuming that such an other-regarding component is large. [In any case] it is not axiomatic in mainstream economics that human beings maximise their own income [and economists – neoliberal or otherwise – do *not*

believe that] people have no other-regarding or social component at all in the utility functions that describe their final choices.

No matter how narrowly we define it, self-interest is clearly a very powerful motivation in human interactions. Towards the end of his chapter on self-interest, Chang acknowledges this, saying, 'Of course, all this is not to deny that self-seeking is one of the most important human motivations' (Chang 2010: 50). It explains why the baker sold bread in the eighteenth century and it continues to explain the bulk of economic behaviour much better than theories based on 'benevolence' or 'lifestyle choices'. However, nobody seriously suggests that it is mankind's only impetus. Altruism, charity and generosity flourish in everyday life and can still be found even in the hard-nosed world of business. As Chang rightly says, 'Self-interest is a most powerful trait in most human beings. However, it's not our only drive' (41). That is the simple truth. No free-market economist has ever said otherwise. On this point, at least, there is no disagreement.

Greed is not good and capitalism does not rely on people being greedy. Capitalism *is* good, however, because it works even when people are greedy.

2 ECONOMISTS BELIEVE PEOPLE ARE PERFECTLY RATIONAL

'Economics is not a science', writes Suzanne Moore in *The Guardian*, 'it's not even a social science. It is an antisocial theory. It assumes behaviour is rational' (Moore 2012). In *The Courageous State*, Richard Murphy (2011: 77) states that economists believe that 'there is perfect information available in markets to inform decisions which are then made optimally. In other words, they assume that we all know everything we need to know about quite literally everything'.

They do not. Rationality is an important concept in economics and economists have different views about the extent to which people are rational, but as Tyler Cowen notes: 'Economists accept no single set of assumptions about rationality, nor any one set of assumptions about the role of rationality assumptions in economic theory and practice' (Cowen 2004: 233). This was highlighted when Eugene Fama and Robert Shiller both won the Nobel Prize in Economics in 2013 despite having starkly different views about the rationality of people and markets. Game theorists tend to assume that people are highly rational, and some theoretical economic models are based on the assumption that individuals are logical and perfectly informed. This does not mean, however, that economists believe that the population is entirely rational, well-informed, intelligent or wise. Nor can the field of economics be demolished with one of the almost infinite number of examples of human foolishness.

Some models are useful

The statistician George E. P. Box once said that 'all models are wrong, but some are useful' (Box and Draper 1987: 424). Theoretical economics sometimes describes a world which no one believes exists, nor ever will exist, and yet it can still be useful. For example, economic theory suggests that, if there is perfect competition in a totally free market, prices will drop to the point at which there is no excess profit. In this scenario, a company sells a product with a ten pence profit margin and so another company jumps in and sells the same product with a nine pence profit margin. This undercutting continues until the product is sold for the exact amount it costs to manufacture, distribute and retail, including the salaries of all involved (the marginal cost of production).

This scenario is patently unrealistic, partly because government regulation precludes the possibility of free markets with total competition and no barriers to entry, but also because in a vibrant and creative economy there are always profit margins for entrepreneurs to chase. But, although the model is hypothetical to a large extent, it contains the important truth that greater competition tends to lead to lower prices. Reducing barriers to entry forces down prices and, all other things being equal, reduces profit margins. As Harris and Seldon (1959: 48) write, '"perfect" competition is a figment of the imagination, although a useful one. It is still true that the less imperfect a market, and the more it approaches the "perfect" model of theory, the better results it might yield in terms of costs and prices.'

It is not necessary for a *totally* free market to exist for the benefits of competition to be shown empirically, nor does a fantasy world of perfect competition have to be created for the benefits of competition to be felt. And it is emphatically not the case that if one pays more than cost price for a product then 'the whole edifice of neoliberal economics collapses', as Richard Murphy claims (Murphy 2011: 45).[1] How different this is from state socialism in which the closer a country gets to the ideal of central planning, the worse the outcomes become (and how ironic that those who criticise the free market for its imperfect competition propose government monopoly as the solution).

---

1   Economists 'assume that every business sells every product it makes at what is called the marginal cost of production. That means all they want back for the product they sell is the precise cost they incur for making the precise item they have sold. So if they sold you, for example, an MP3 download then they not only should but must, if this model of utopia described by neoliberal economists is to work, charge you just exactly what it cost them to make the MP3 download they sold to you. I kid you not: the whole edifice of neoliberal economics and the mantra so often repeated that business is more efficient than government is based on this type of logic.' (Murphy 2011: 44–45).

To take an example from Econ 101, a model which assumes that lower prices will lead to more sales is useful, not because the outcome *invariably* follows the intervention, but because it will *tend* to do so, has been *shown* to do so and there are common sense reasons why it *should* do so. Similarly, a model which assumes that people make rational, self-interested decisions is useful, not because people invariably do so, but because most people try to do so, and frequently succeed in doing so, most of the time. Rational man, or *homo economicus,* 'is not only a simplification of man, as all models will be, but he is also a caricature for he epitomises to an extreme degree the essential characteristics of economic behaviour' (Morgan 1996: 20). So long as the caricature represents a fundamental truth about how people tend to behave, the model is useful.

Rational choice and behavioural economics

A fair degree of rationality can be expected from human beings. As P. J. O'Rourke says, it would be most peculiar if we consistently acted irrationally: 'Imagine a world where we went about our daily activities deliberately intending not to profit by them – eating pebbles, wooing the furniture, getting into our car for the sole purpose of driving into a tree' (O'Rourke 2007: 50–51). Predictions based on logical utility maximisation can be tested empirically. Suzanne Moore may be right when she says that economics is not science, but it *is* a social science. It studies human activity, and therefore can never predict behaviour with the precision with which we associate the natural sciences.

Nevertheless, we can observe behaviour and make reasonable predictions about what most people would do in routine situations based on their rational self-interest.

In mainstream economics, rationality 'simply means that people behave in ways consistent with their preferences' (Parkin et al. 2013). Behaving rationally means 'choosing the best means to the chooser's ends' (Posner 1998). The task of economists would be so much easier if the world was populated with clear-headed, far-sighted, logical utility maximisers. Alas, it is not and few, if any, mainstream economists endorse a dogmatic version of rational choice theory in which people are assumed to be cold, calculating machines. Far from having a simplistic view of humanity, economists have relentlessly challenged and undermined the notion of 'rational man' for decades (Simon 1955; Sen 1977). Such concepts as 'bounded rationality', 'rational ignorance' and 'rational irrationality' have emerged from within the profession, with economists such as Richard Thaler, Vernon Smith, Ariel Rubinstein, Cass Sunstein, Ronald Coase and Bryan Caplan being among the contributors, assisted by a few psychologists, notably Daniel Kahneman and Dan Ariely. The whole field of behavioural economics has been testing the limits of rational behaviour for years while producing best-selling books and Nobel laureates. This is not some obscure sect challenging the conventional wisdom of rational man.

Behavioural economists have shown that many decisions are swayed by unconscious and irrational biases which result in people falling short of their goal of maximising their utility. Moreover, they have shown that – for some people, at least – these biases are systematic and predictable. We are, they say, predictably irrational (Ariely 2009). We are prone to irrational biases such as the gambler's fallacy[2] and the lightning-never-strikes-twice fallacy. We suffer from loss aversion[3] and are susceptible to the madness of crowds. We allow ourselves to be influenced by others, especially when they tell us what we want to hear (confirmation bias). We are liable to expect current trends to continue and to forget previous losses (the new paradigm fallacy). We tend to put an exaggerated value on the present compared with the future (hyperbolic discounting) and even those of us who reject superstition are liable to chase financial losses, or be caught up in market bubbles, or act impulsively due to anger, love or pity. It can be argued that much 'irrational' behaviour is actually due to a lack of information rather than a deficit of logic – people tend to over-estimate the odds of being murdered or dying in a plane crash, for example (Posner 1998: 1573) – but there are enough examples of self-defeating irrationality to make us doubt rational choice theory in its most rigid form.

These are all interesting and potentially useful observations, but mainstream economists have never claimed that people are infallible. Supporters of rational choice theory, such as Gary Becker and Richard Posner, do not believe that models which assume a large degree of rationality are

---

2   The belief that the outcome of a random event, such as a coin toss, is affected by previous outcomes of the same event.

3   Preferring to avoid a loss rather than make a gain.

threatened by insights from behavioural economics, many of which have been incorporated into their work (Herfeld 2012). 'The rational-choice economist asks what "rational man" would do in a given situation,' writes Posner, 'and usually the answer is pretty clear and it can be confirmed. Sometimes it is not confirmed – and so we have behavioural economics' (Posner 1998: 1559). In the absence of a more compelling theory, they say, a model which assumes that people try to choose the best means to achieve their ends has greater predictive and explanatory power than any other – it is good enough to be *useful*. But they also note that economists 'long ago abandoned the model of hyperrational, emotionless, unsocial, supremely egoistic, nonstrategic man (or woman)' (ibid.: 1552). Like his close relative, the selfish capitalist, rational man is made of straw.

Have we found angels to govern us?

Debating mankind's quotient of rationality may seem like an arcane academic exercise, but there is a practical issue at stake. For free-market economists, the question is not whether people are perfectly informed, impeccably rational individuals – obviously they are not – but whether they are better placed to make informed and rational decisions for themselves than politicians and bureaucrats are on their behalf. Criticism of the rational man hypothesis often leads to the conclusion that the government should intervene more strongly when rationality runs dry and information is imperfect. Ha-Joon Chang, for example, jumps seamlessly from straw man to statism in *23 Things They Don't Tell You About Capitalism*, asking 'how can we accept economic theories that work only because they assume that people are fully rational? The upshot is that we are simply not smart enough to leave the market alone' (Chang 2010: 173). By this, he means that 'we' (the people) are not smart enough and so 'we' (the government) must intervene.

The psychologist and behavioural economist Dan Ariely strikes a similar chord in his book *Predictably Irrational*. After describing some experiments which show that the price people are prepared to pay for certain goods can be manipulated, Ariely (2009: 48) concludes as follows:

> So, where does this leave us? If we can't rely on the market forces of supply and demand to set optimal market prices, and we can't count on free-market mechanisms to help us maximise our utility, then we may need to look elsewhere. This is especially the case with society's essentials, such as health care, medicine, water, electricity, education, and other critical resources. If you accept the premise that market forces and free markets will not always regulate the market for the best, then you may find yourself among those who believe that the government (we hope a reasonable and thoughtful government) must play a larger role in regulating some market activities, even if this limits free enterprise. Yes, a free market based on supply, demand, and no friction would be ideal if we were truly rational. Yet when we are not rational but irrational, policies should take this important factor into account.

The problem with delegating power from the individual to the state in the way Chang and Ariely propose is that the government is made up of the same flawed men and women who are supposedly so irrational in the market-place. It is far from clear that we can expect the government to be 'reasonable and thoughtful' and there are few, if any, historical precedents for the state setting 'optimal market prices'. Furthermore, if consumers suffer from systematic bias, so do voters. Can we expect irrational politicians elected by irrational voters to be more rational than the average Joe? In a famous rhetorical question posed in his first inaugural address in 1801, Thomas Jefferson (2001: 5) suggested that we could not:

> Sometimes it is said that man cannot be trusted with the government of himself. Can he then be trusted with the government of others? Or have we found angels, in the form of kings, to govern him?

If buyers, sellers and politicians were all equally irrational, it might make little difference who makes decisions in an economy, but there are reasons to think that politicians' decisions will often be worse. Their incentives to seek the best outcomes for the electorate are weaker than the incentives individuals have to advance their own interests themselves. They are surrounded by vested interests trying to persuade them to pass laws that will benefit a minority at the expense of the majority. And even if the politician can gather together an elite team of wiser persons who are objectively more rational than the man on the Clapham omnibus, he cannot possibly know the varied preferences of every citizen.

Consider how politicians come to wield power in the first place. They are elected, generally with less than half of the popular vote,[4] by an electorate that is not entirely rational and is largely ignorant of politics and economics. Bryan Caplan argues that it would not greatly matter if the majority of voters were ignorant and irrational since they would vote in an essentially random manner in which their votes are cancelled out, leaving an informed minority as kingmakers who would swing the election towards the candidate with the best policies. However, he says that the situation is even worse than that. Voters are not just ignorant, they are misguided and systematically biased towards bad policies.

Over a period of many years, voters have been shown to support a range of policies which economists from across the political spectrum agree are costly and counter-productive. A worrying number of non-economists continue to hold beliefs which Caplan describes as 'positively silly' such as the notion that technology destroys jobs and that trading with other countries is bad for the economy (the latter objection usually being framed in terms of 'jobs being sent overseas'). It is not unusual, even in broadsheet newspapers, to be told that crime and disease are good for the economy because they create work for those who

---

4   In 2005, the Labour government had a large working majority with around 35 per cent of the popular vote and with just over 20 per cent of the electorate voting for it.

have to clear up the mess – a fallacy that was mocked by economists in the mid-nineteenth century (Bastiat 1995). At the most elementary level, very large numbers of voters and politicians are wedded to ancient misconceptions about economics which can most generously be described as only superficially appealing.

The basics of economics, as explained in Adam Smith's *Wealth of Nations*, are not hard to grasp and may even seem obvious, but, as Caplan (2007: 32) points out, people needed to hear them in 1776 and have needed to hear them ever since:

> If Adam Smith's observations are only truisms, why did he bother to write them? Why do teachers of economics keep quoting and re-quoting this passage [about people naturally being led to 'employment which is most advantageous to society']? *Because Smith's thesis was counterintuitive to his contemporaries, and remains counterintuitive today.* [Emphasis in original]

Take the issue of employment, for example. Individuals clearly benefit from having a job and need to have no understanding of economics to be incentivised to find one, but when economically naive politicians make it their task to find work for others, they are liable to endorse immigration controls, bailouts of failing companies, protectionism for failing industries and 'job creation' in the public sector (the only sector that they can easily control). Economists have understood for centuries that such policies are unsound. Although protectionism and tariffs appear to 'create' or 'safeguard' jobs, such policies encourage unproductive employment which drains the economy. Nevertheless, such schemes continue to be politically popular.

None of this should be construed as an argument for giving economists supreme executive power, let alone allowing capitalists to run rampant ('The government of an exclusive company of merchants,' wrote Smith (1999: 152), 'is, perhaps, the worst of all governments'). The point about the free market is that it does not require central direction. Individuals do not need to understand the economic system in which they live for it to work. They know enough about their own abilities and aspirations to work productively in their occupation of choice. The problems only come about when authorities devise well-meaning schemes to help them out, often as a result of irrational voters electing badly informed politicians who pander to special interests and ill-informed prejudices.

Individuals rarely have perfect information, but collectively they have vastly more information about local circumstances and personal wants than any government agency could hope to gather. Once we recognise that the state is run by fallible human beings who have been elected by other fallible human beings, the case for the state making decisions for millions of people – who have different goals, different interests and different abilities – ceases to be attractive except when there is no reasonable alternative. 'The law ought to trust people with the care of their own interest', wrote Adam Smith, because 'they must generally be able to judge better of it than the legislator can do' (Smith 1999: 110).

Rational consumers and irrational voters

Critics of free markets believe that they have spotted a contradiction between economists' belief in rational individuals in the marketplace and irrational individuals in a democracy – a paradox satirically characterised by one commentator as 'everyone is rational, except policy-makers' (Quiggin 2010: 107). At first glance, this seems to be as incoherent as socialists' faith in rational government and irrational markets. Why would a rational consumer suddenly become irrational when he enters a voting booth?

The answer is simple and, like so much economics, it comes down to incentives. Voters have little incentive to be knowledgeable about politics and – crucially – *can afford to be wrong*. A single vote almost never decides an election. The individual can cast his vote in the near-certain know-ledge that it will make no difference to the result. He has scant incentive to vote at all, let alone to read up on each and every policy the candidates claim to stand for. Many people *do* vote, of course, perhaps out of a sense of duty or to express themselves, but the opportunity cost of voting is trivial – a few minutes going to the polls or filling out a postal vote[5] – whereas the effort required in mastering the issues is enormous. An ill-informed decision at the ballot box has practically no private cost to the individual. Even

---

5 Despite this, evidence suggests that many people do not place a great value on their vote. More than a third of registered voters did not cast a ballot in the last UK general election. The fact that bad weather reduces voter turnout implies that some people think their vote is worth less than a relatively trivial opportunity cost.

in the extremely unlikely event of his vote being decisive, the costs of electing a fool or a knave will be dispersed over a large population. In short, voters can afford to indulge their irrational impulses at virtually zero cost every few years.

This is very different from being irrational with one's own money in the market. A poor decision in the marketplace will cost us our hard-earned money. A mistake at work might cost us our job. It is because the private costs of making a bad choice are so much greater when our own money is at stake that we are incentivised to gather information and choose carefully when making a purchase in the marketplace. The more expensive the item, the greater the incentive we have to educate ourselves about what we are buying. In financial transactions, it is rational to spend time gathering knowledge about the options. In politics, unless you are a journalist, politician or lobbyist, it is rational to ignore the whole circus and spend one's time more productively. 'Voting is not a slight variation on shopping,' says Caplan (2007: 140–41). 'Shoppers have incentives to be rational. Voters do not.' There is, therefore, no contradiction between being a rational actor in the market and an irrational or ignorant participant (or abstainer) in a democracy.

Conclusion

There is no assumption in mainstream economics that people are perfectly rational and it is quite absurd to suggest that 'neoliberal economists assume that human beings when engaging in the market place are omniscient: they can clairvoyantly foretell everything that might happen and how likely it is to occur and when' (Murphy 2011: 37).

Economists do not see a world populated by totally irrational voters, wholly self-serving politicians and perfectly informed consumers. Selfishness, ignorance, altruism and reason are fairly evenly distributed among the population. A fool in a polling booth does not become a sage in a shopping centre and a corrupt politician does not become Francis of Assisi when he sets up a small business. The extent to which we seek out information and behave rationally depends on the incentives we are given and the costs of acting foolishly. As voters, the cost of irrationality and ignorance is practically zero. As agents in the market, the cost is much greater and we respond accordingly. 'Assuming that all people are fully rational all the time is bad economics,' writes Caplan (2007: 135). 'It makes more sense to assume that people tailor their degree of rationality to the costs of error.'

Free-market economists do not assume that individuals always know what is best for them, but they *do* assume that individuals are better placed to know their own preferences than a distant bureaucrat. So long as we bear the consequences of our actions, the path of progress is better trod by sovereign beings pursuing their goals through voluntary cooperation than by a technocratic elite prodding us all in the same direction.

3 ECONOMISTS THINK GDP IS ALL THAT MATTERS

'It's time we admitted that there's more to life than money,' said David Cameron in 2006, while still the leader of the parliamentary opposition, 'and it's time we focused not just on GDP, but on GWB – general well-being' (BBC 2006). In this, Cameron was echoing the words of Tony Blair, who wrote in 1999: 'Money isn't everything. But in the past governments have seemed to forget this. Success has been measured by economic growth – GDP – alone' (Easton 2006).

Both political leaders were tapping into a widely held belief that British society had become obsessed with increasing national income at the expense of the good life. According to this narrative, the neoliberal counter-revolution of Margaret Thatcher and Ronald Reagan had focused exclusively on the creation of wealth. In their blinkered materialism, advocates of free markets pursued money in the belief that it would make them happy. The production and consumption of goods had become the sole goal of public policy and all efforts were judged by whether they increased Gross Domestic Product.

Sometimes this obsession is put in terms of disease, addiction, religion or pathology. We are 'addicted to growth', according to the Centre for the Advancement of a Steady State Economy (Gardner 2011). The economist Joseph Stiglitz has urged politicians to 'get away from GDP fetishism' (Jolly 2009). In a reference to Alcoholics Anonymous, the campaign group Post Growth offers a twelve step programme to 'treat our growth addiction' (Nelson 2010) while Andrew Simms of the New Economics Foundation says that 'the "call to prayer" of conventional economics has been the incantation of economic growth figures' (Simms 2009). For Stephen Lacey of Climate Progress, GDP 'is the crack-cocaine of economic indicators' which 'fits in perfectly with society's single-minded obsession with growth' (Lacey 2012). George Monbiot writes of 'the iron god of growth to which we must bow' (Monbiot 2013) while Oxfam's Economic Justice Policy Officer complains about 'the "growth at all costs" neoliberal mantra of the last 30-odd years' (Oxfam GB 2012).

It is a powerful narrative. The only thing missing is an example of any economist or politician ever expressing support for the 'growth at all costs' mantra which has supposedly been the global doctrine of capitalism for several decades. Cameron and Blair both saw themselves as challenging the conventional wisdom and yet it is surprisingly difficult to track down advocates of the alleged orthodoxy. It may be that some people truly believe that GDP is the only measure of success, as Blair claimed. Perhaps they genuinely think that there is nothing more to life than money, as Cameron asserted. But if so, they have kept their thoughts to themselves. Public discussion about national income almost invariably centres on the more credible assertion that GDP is not a measure of anything other than economic output and that money does not necessarily buy you happiness.

It is doubtful whether anyone has ever viewed GDP as the be-all and end-all. Simon Kuznets, the economist who invented GDP as a measure, told the US Congress in the 1930s that 'the welfare of a nation can ... scarcely be inferred from a measure of national income as defined by the GDP' (Faris 2009). Many years later Robert Kennedy (1968) delivered a famous speech in which he addressed the limits of gross national product:

> Yet the gross national product does not allow for the health of our children, the quality of their education, or the joy of their play. It does not include the beauty of our poetry or the strength of our marriages; the intelligence of our public debate or the integrity of our public officials. It measures neither our wit nor our courage; neither our wisdom nor our learning; neither our compassion nor our devotion to our country; it measures everything, in short, except that which makes life worthwhile. And it tells us everything about America except why we are proud that we are Americans.

Then, as now, it was not clear to whom this rebuke was being directed. Even among economists, GDP is not seen as the only, or even necessarily the main, indicator of economic progress. Statistics pertaining to unemployment, inflation, debt, inequality, wages and the balance of trade have all preoccupied economic strategists to a lesser or greater extent in the last century. In 1944, Friedrich Hayek – a free-market economist if ever there was one – shared the consensus view when he said that 'the conquest of unemployment' was 'the one aim which everybody now agrees comes in the front rank' of economic priorities (Hayek 2001: 211). Throughout the Thatcher era, the averagely well-informed newspaper reader was more likely to have had a better idea of what the current unemployment and inflation figures were than to know the last quarter's GDP growth rate.

A blind obsession?

Perhaps we do not need to identify a specific individual who espouses the 'growth at all costs mantra' for such an attitude to be the implicit doctrine of government. Politicians from Kennedy to Cameron might deny that they are smitten with GDP, but their actions may betray them. In other words, there may not literally be a temple to the god of economic growth, but our leaders pray to it all the same.

This argument does not stand up against the facts. If 'growth at all costs' were truly the mantra of the last thirty years, we would expect this to be reflected in policy. If society has a 'blind obsession with growth' (Peck 2012), as the New Economics Foundation claims, we should have seen massive deregulation, open borders immigration, huge tax cuts, looser planning laws, the abolition of subsidies and the withering away of the state. Instead, we have seen

Figure 1 **Public spending in 2013/14 prices (UK)**

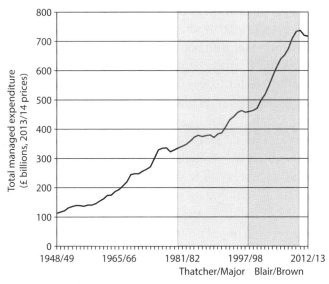

Source: IFS (2014).

bureaucracies expand, regulations spread and taxes rise. Public spending in the UK more than doubled in real terms during the era of supposed neoliberalism, from £337 billion in 1979/80 to £735 billion by the end of the last decade (see Figure 1, inflation-adjusted to 2013/14 prices).[1]

These data are more commonly shown as percentages of GDP, which have ranged from 35 per cent (in the mid

---

1   The government was already spending £654 billion in 2006/07 before the economy slowed down. The coalition government's 'austerity' programme intends to reduce spending to £685 billion by 2016/17.

1950s) to 48 per cent (in the mid 1970s). Since GDP has risen enormously since World War II, showing spending as a percentage of national income tends to downplay the scale of increase, with some left-wing commentators portraying budget cuts relative to GDP as being cuts in real terms (Hutton 2013). It is, however, far from obvious that public spending should always rise in line with economic growth. On the contrary, a state that provides only essential services would be expected to spend a smaller share of national income as the economy expands, in the same way that a family spends a smaller share of its income on essentials as it becomes wealthier. That has clearly not happened in the UK in the past sixty years, where a 30 per cent increase in population size has been accompanied by a 600 per cent rise in government spending.

Throughout this period of state expansion, most of the policies that were enacted breezily disregarded economic growth in the pursuit of higher goals such as health and safety, climate change, child protection, workers' rights, literacy, life expectancy, diversity, equality and environmentalism. All of these can stake a more plausible claim to be the obsession of modern government.

Only in recent years, with the global recession weighing heavily on politicians' minds, has economic growth explicitly become the number one priority for both left and right. In the long period of prosperity that preceded the financial crisis there was a contrarian revolt against economic growth, largely from the political left, which portrayed GDP as a false idol and proposed a 'steady-state' (i.e. zero growth) economy as the ecologically friendly and morally upright alternative. At its extreme, it inspired articles such as 'Bring on the recession' (George Monbiot, *The Guardian*, 2007), 'Bring on the pain of a recession and purge our coarsened souls' (Tim Lott, *The Independent*, 2008), and 'Hurrah for the recession. It will do us a power of good' (Hephzibah Anderson, *The Observer*, 2008). For a brief period before the impact of economic decline kicked in, scarcity and want were portrayed as noble ends. Recession would, it was hoped, 'force us to recall the thrill of yearning for something, the more tantalising aspects of restraint, the delicious frisson of anticipation rather than the dull ache of satiation' (Anderson 2008).

This disdain for growth lost is allure in the barren years that followed. The French President Nicholas Sarkozy reportedly delayed publication of a report which called for well-being to replace GDP as a measure of success because 'he thought discussing happiness in the depths of the economic crisis might have been unpopular' (Samuel 2009). He was probably right. The newspaper columnists who had beckoned in the recession were strangely silent when the economy tanked in the years that followed and even Britain's most outspoken steady-staters, the New Economics Foundation, whose publications included *Growth Isn't Working* (2006) and *Growth Isn't Possible* (2010), muted their opposition to growth during the downturn. In January 2010, they had asserted that 'economic growth is no longer possible for rich countries' (NEF 2010), but after a Conservative-led coalition was elected a few months later, the think tank repeatedly criticised government policy for failing to engineer growth and complained that 'austerity kills recovery' (Meadway 2012). The arch anti-consumerists bemoaned the fact that consumer spending had fallen more sharply than in any previous recession and denounced 'George Osborne's obsessive commitment to austerity' (Peck 2012).[2]

For a while during the Great Recession, there was an urgent political consensus for growth, and yet the pro-growth policies of the period only served to illustrate that GDP was a second-order priority at other times. To give one example, in September 2012 the government announced that it would temporarily relax planning restrictions and health and safety regulations in order to boost economic growth (BBC 2012; Savage et al. 2012). This was a tacit acknowledgement that such laws restrict GDP and are not wholly necessary, but there was no suggestion that they would be abolished on a permanent basis. Once the economy could afford them again, they would be reinstated.

---

2 It might seem perverse for left-wing critics to be anti-growth one minute and pro-growth the next but, as Revel (1977: 156) pointed out forty years ago, their real aim is to attack the market economy whatever the circumstances: 'Until 1973, after twenty years of expansion with full employment and moderate inflation, the mortal illness of capitalism was – inevitably – growth. After that it became stagnation. Before, capitalism was burning up the planet's resources while alienating humanity through overconsumption; after, it was fading into the doldrums while starving the third world. Not that the diatribes of Western socialists changed from one period to the next; the same severity of language was used to denounce all types of error in all its forms.'

No design for life

Much of the criticism directed at economics stems from a sense that it lacks a moral centre – that it does not tell us how we should live. Robert A. Johnson, executive director of the Institute for New Economic Thinking, has a point when he accuses economists of being 'devoid of answers' to such questions as 'What is a meaningful life?' and 'What do we aspire to?' (Johnson 2012). The shortcomings of GDP as a measure of a nation can equally be applied to economics generally. It is true that GDP cannot quantify 'those unpriced but priceless services carried out by domestic workers and by nature' (Gleeson-White 2012). It is true, as Robert Kennedy said, that it 'measures neither our wit nor our courage'.

But it is also true that the Richter scale measures neither wit nor courage, and voltage does not tell us what to aspire to, and yet seismology and physics somehow escape criticism for these shortcomings. Economists do not claim to have created a formula for the good life or to have found a unifying theory of everything. The function of many criticisms of economics is to caricature free marketeers as narrow-minded materialists whose bleak view of humanity contrasts starkly with the thoughtful, holistic folk who have been bestowed with the insight that there is more to life than money. The challengers to the supposed conventional wisdom have a 'philosophy' while the economists have only an 'ideology' (or perhaps a religion – those who believe in the free movement of goods and labour are sometimes termed 'free-market fundamentalists'). In this narrative, free-market economists are not only obsessed with material possessions, but, in their thirst for wealth and consumption, ignore human well-being and are blind to the negative aspects of growth, such as environmental pollution. By putting a price tag on everything (including whole nations, hence GDP) it is supposed that they forget that some things cannot be bought and sold.

This is a straw man and the underlying premise is inane. Far from being free thinking iconoclasts, critics of materialism are echoing clichés that go back centuries. 'What is the point of walls and warships and glittering statues if the men who build them are not happy?' asked Socrates in the fifth century BC. 'Nought's had, all's spent/Where our desire is got without content', spoke Lady Macbeth. 'I don't care too much for money/Money can't buy me love', sang The Beatles. Philosophers, prophets, politicians and pop stars have been making the same point since the dawn of time. Being clichés doesn't make them untrue (clichés are usually true), but when the same sentiments are expressed by everyone from Socrates to Sarkozy via Jesus Christ, Paul McCartney and Tony Blair, one must conclude that 'there's more to life than money' is not a dazzling new profundity but is itself the conventional wisdom.

Economics does not seek to challenge these sentiments. It is not a rival to religion or philosophy. It does not tell people how they should behave, nor does it dictate what priorities society should have. Economics is, as the dictionary defines it, 'the science of the production and distribution of wealth'. GDP has never been anything more than a measurement of national wealth, but measuring a nation's wealth surely has a place in a field of study devoted to its production and distribution. While there are valid criticisms to be made of GDP as a gauge of economic output, it remains the best measure available to us for the clearly limited purpose for which it was designed.

Conclusion

No economist thinks that GDP is the sole measure of an economy, let alone of a society, nor do they believe it is a measure of well-being. It is true that free-market policies create economic growth more effectively than any other system, and many would argue that this is reason enough to implement them, but it does not follow that economists idolise GDP, nor that free marketeers regard growth as paramount.

GDP was 'not designed as a measure of individual or national well-being' (Office for National Statistics 2012a: 3). It is no more than a measure of output and so it is naturally of great interest to economists. The many benefits of economic growth (which we will discuss in Chapter 7) are sufficient to warrant a close eye being kept on it, but that does not make free-market economists 'evangelical worshippers' of GDP (Nordhaus and Tobin 1972: 4).

The point of the free market is not to create wealth per se – although that is a welcome side effect – but to provide 'freedom for people to buy what they want from whoever they please' (Norberg 2003: 128). This includes the freedom to live in a commune and eat nothing but humous if that is their preference. It is a myth that free-market economists believe that 'everything that indicates success in life depends on consuming more', as Richard Murphy (2011: 12) insists they do. As Michael Prowse (1998: 391) writes:

> Allowing individuals to make as many choices as possible for themselves is not an argument for greed or materialism. For all I care, everyone can spend their days meditating or tending their gardens. I do not care if the GDP shrinks. What matters is that the pattern of activity reflects people's free choices.

Unlike progressives and state socialists, free-market economists do not have a prescription for the good life. This is sometimes held against them by those who have grander plans for remodelling society.

4 ECONOMISTS THINK WE LIVE IN A FREE MARKET

In *23 Things They Don't Tell You About Capitalism*, Ha-Joon Chang argues that modern capitalist economies are not free markets. '[T]he free market is an illusion', he says. 'If some markets *look* free, it is only because we so totally accept the regulations that are propping them up that they become invisible' (Chang 2010: 3 – emphasis in the original). He cites laws against child labour and slavery, limits on industrial pollution and restrictions on the sale of alcohol, firearms and medicines to demonstrate that 'carefully examined, markets are revealed to be propped up by rules – and many of them' (ibid.: 4). He mentions goods and services that cannot legally be bought and sold, such as human organs, illicit drugs, electoral votes, government appointments and legal judgements. Furthermore, he argues that immigration controls and minimum wage legislation mean that 'all our wages are, at root, politically determined' (ibid.: 5).

A free market is not anarchy

Chang has a point. Because the free market does not require central planning by government, it is easy to characterise capitalism as being the *absence* of systems and rules. This is a mistake. There are plenty of rules and regulations that free marketeers want to get rid of, but there are many laws that are essential for capitalism to function. So does the existence of rules mean that the free market is 'an illusion'? This is so only if your idea of a free market is a land without laws.

Chang seems to think that a market cannot be free if it is 'propped up by rules'. He conflates free markets with a Hobbesian state of nature. Free-market economists make it abundantly clear that rules of a certain form are necessary to protect freedom, encourage enterprise and foster competition. It is important to have laws to protect property rights and to prevent monopoly and dishonest advertising. Legally binding agreements must be honoured and contract law must be enforced. All this requires government action. 'The existence of a free market does not of course eliminate the need for government,' wrote Milton Friedman. 'On the contrary, government is essential both as a forum for determining the "rules of the game" and as an umpire to interpret and enforce the rules decided on' (Friedman 2002: 15).

The question is not whether there should be rules, but what those rules should be. Some laws are helpful and necessary, others are wasteful and superfluous. It is not a matter of being 'pro-regulation' or 'anti-regulation'. One of the most pervasive myths about free-market economics, reflected in Chang's critique, is that it demands laissez-faire. In 1944, Friedrich Hayek complained that 'probably nothing has done so much harm to the liberal cause than the wooden insistence of some liberals on certain rough rules of thumb, above all the principle of laissez-faire' (Hayek 2001: 18). Instead, Hayek argued that people must be free to buy and sell from anyone at any agreed price and that there should be no artificial barriers to trade, no price controls and no legal discrimination. This, however, is not laissez-faire and it is certainly not anarchy. He continued (Hayek 2001: 39):

> The functioning of competition not only requires adequate organisation of certain institutions like money, markets, and channels of information – some of which can never be adequately provided by private enterprise – but it depends above all on the existence of an appropriate legal system, a legal system designed both to preserve competition and to make it operate as beneficially as possible.

Among the tasks which can only be carried out by government, Hayek included regulation of industry and what we would now call health and safety (ibid.: 39):

> To prohibit the use of certain poisonous substances, or to require special precautions in their use, to limit working hours or to require certain sanitary arrangements, is fully compatible with the preservation of competition. The only question here is whether in the particular instance the advantages gained are greater than the social costs which they impose.

Milton Friedman made much the same point when he wrote *Capitalism and Freedom* (Friedman 2002: 32):

> Our principles offer no hard and fast line how far it is appropriate to use government to accomplish jointly what is difficult or impossible for us to accomplish separately through strictly voluntary exchange. In any particular case of proposed intervention, we must make up a balance sheet, listing separately the advantages and disadvantages.

Clearly, free-market economists believe that regulations are necessary and that the ultimate test is, as Hayek says, whether 'the advantages gained are greater than the social costs which they impose.' From Smith to Friedman, objections to state interference in private industry have not been rooted in some fundamentalist obsession with whittling away the state – although others have made the argument for a minimal state on philosophical grounds (e.g. Nozick 1974) – but because over-regulation frequently increases costs, stifles innovation and fails to solve the problems it sets out to address.

Hayek accepted that there are some goods, such as signposts and roads, which are best supplied by the collective. Upon occasions when 'the conditions for the proper working of competition cannot be created' we must 'resort to the substitution of direct regulation by authority.' The word 'resort' implies that a competitive free market is preferable to state monopoly, and so it is, but there nevertheless remains a 'wide and unquestioned field for state activity.

In no system that could be rationally defended would the state just do nothing' (Hayek 2001: 40). The question, then, is how much the state should do.

Capitalists don't like free markets

Chang says that the market economy has the appearance of being free 'only because we so unconditionally accept its underlying restrictions that we fail to see them' (Chang 2010: 1). But free-market economists *do* see them and they often challenge them. Far from being one of the things 'they don't tell you about capitalism', free-market economists continually point out that we do not live in a free market, not because they desire a lawless state of nature but because they believe that regulations are often unnecessary, including several of the laws which Chang says we 'unconditionally accept'. There are strong social and economic arguments for legalising the sale of narcotics and human organs, for example (Meadowcroft 2008). Many free-market economists oppose minimum wage laws and immigration controls, and some have made the case against bans on child labour, particularly in countries where there is extreme poverty and no schools (Norberg 2003: 1999). Plenty of people support ending the war on drugs, or removing the minimum wage, or allowing the free movement of labour between countries, but supporters of a market economy are perhaps the only people who tend to hold all three of these views simultaneously.

The thrust of Chang's critique is that capitalists embrace regulation when it suits them, but complain about 'politically motivated interference' when their profits are threatened. As it happens, most of the regulatory examples Chang offers do not unequivocally benefit capitalists. On the contrary, it is quite conceivable that businessmen could have more money-making opportunities if they could sell slaves or employ children in heavily polluting methamphetamine labs. The laws he mentions have generally come about as a result of lobbying from an assortment of conservatives, socialists, environmentalists and 'concerned citizens', rather than by rent-seeking industrialists.

Nevertheless, it is not difficult to come up with an alternative list of regulations which have been created to benefit big business. Chang is quite right to draw attention to the influence of special interests, including commercial interests, in the creation of laws. He is quite wrong, however, to imply that supporters of a free market are comfortable with this. His mistake is to conflate capitalism – or a certain type of capitalism – with a free market.[1] For more than 200 years, economists have complained that capitalists, or business interests, are among the free market's greatest foes. 'Business corporations in general are not defenders of free enterprise,' wrote Milton Friedman in 1978,

---

[1] This confusion begins with his book's title: *23 Things They Don't Tell You About Capitalism*. Throughout the book, it is clear that 'they' are free-market economists, and yet the 'things they don't tell you' involve criticisms that free-market economists have been voicing for many years. It is absurd to suggest that free-market economists believe that Africa cannot develop without foreign aid (Chapter 11), that the world's poor are less entrepreneurial than Westerners (Chapter 15) and that bailing out General Motors is to be applauded (Chapter 18).

'On the contrary, they are one of the chief sources of danger' (Friedman 1978). Adam Smith famously complained that 'People of the same trade seldom meet together, even for merriment and diversion, but the conversation ends in a conspiracy against the public, or in some contrivance to raise prices' (Smith 1957: 117).

One of the central themes of *The Wealth of Nations* is the ceaseless attempt of business interests or capitalists to protect their profits by persuading legislators to create new laws ('rent-seeking'). The narrow self-interest of wealthy businessmen often lies in excluding competitors, fixing prices and raising barriers to entry. They disguise their self-interest with the cloak of the 'public interest'. The brewer calls for higher taxes on spirits to protect the public health. The baker calls for tariffs on imported bread to protect jobs. But it is the public who pay the price for these regulations and, as Smith explained, 'the interest of the State and the nation is constantly sacrificed to that of some particular class of traders' (Smith 1957: 156).

Few on the political left struggle to accept the notion that big business can have a malign influence on the body politic. However, it is not only organised capital, but organised labour, organised ideologues and organised bureaucrats who can lead a 'conspiracy against the public'. State monopolies are at least as inefficient as private monopolies, and government itself is a monopoly. Politicians and bureaucrats are able to enrich themselves at the public's expense. Trade unions exist, in large part, to raise the price of labour – and therefore the price of goods and services – through closed shops and industrial action. The guilds of Adam Smith's day restricted entry into the professions by limiting apprenticeships. Large corporations today often welcome heavy regulation because it raises barriers to entry for fledgling companies that cannot afford to abide by it.

All these groups are motivated by self-interest and all require the help and protection of the state to maximise their profits and profile. Furthermore, self-interest is not always pecuniary and there are numerous pressure groups who seek special privileges for ideological reasons. P. J. O'Rourke (2007: 77) cites a personal example:

> In rural New England where I live, the conservative preservationist kooks, who want every 7-Eleven replaced with a collapsing barn, join amiably with the liberal back-to-nature dopes, who think highway potholes should be protected as wetland resources. Together they have ensured that it's an hour's drive to the nearest Wal-Mart.

In each and every case, the result of anti-competitive special pleading is to raise prices, or – in the case of government action – to raise taxes; taxes being the price of government. The damage done by rent-seeking legislation cannot be undone by yet more regulation. The answer lies in fostering competition. Although 'people of the same trade' can organise price-fixing conspiracies, these cannot long endure in a competitive market. So long as barriers to entry are low, new entrants can undercut the cartel. Even if such barriers are high, each of the conspirators faces the daily temptation of leaving the cartel to make the handsome profits that would come from undercutting his rivals.

Such conspiracies and contrivances depend on merchants persuading legislators to regulate in their favour. Smith accepted that banning meetings between merchants would not be compatible with a free society, but he said that the law 'ought to do nothing to facilitate such assemblies; much less to render them necessary' (Smith 1957: 117). As Butler writes, paraphrasing Adam Smith: 'The only truly effective discipline over businesses is their fear of losing customers. A competitive market in which customers are sovereign is a surer way to regulate their behaviour than any number of official rules – which so often produce the opposite of their avowed intention' (Butler 2007: 27). Or, as O'Rourke puts it: 'The wise enemy of Wal-Mart wants one right in town – with a Target next door' (O'Rourke 2007: 78).

No free-market economist from Smith onwards has had a rose-tinted vision of the capitalist as philanthropist. It is competition for customers and workers that 'restrains his frauds and corrects his negligence' (Smith 1957: 117). Because the capitalist is not the natural friend of free and open markets, the law must foster competition by ignoring his pleas for protectionism and rent-seeking, preventing the creation of monopolies and cartels, and outlawing anti-competitive practices such as price-fixing and predatory pricing. These are regulations, without question, but they are regulations which are entirely compatible with a free market. There is little incentive to build up a business in countries where contracts are not enforced by law and property is arbitrarily confiscated. Such laws were enforced in eighteenth-century Britain and Adam Smith (1999: 120) said that the 'security which the laws in Great Britain give to every man that he shall enjoy the fruits of his own labour, is alone sufficient to make any country flourish.' The aim of the free market is not to eliminate all regulation, but to foster competition, innovation and efficiency.

Planning, private and public

After making the argument that the existence of rules means that the free market is an illusion, Chang claims that 'we are still living in planned economies' (Chang 2010: 199). This extraordinary claim is based on little more than sophistry. Chang accepts that there is less central planning in most economies than there was thirty years ago, but he points out that companies tend to have business plans and 'a CEO is expected to be a "man (or a woman) with a *plan*"' (Chang 2010: 208 – emphasis in the original). 'Businesses plan their activities,' he writes, 'often down to the last detail' (ibid.). This is unarguable, but the existence of business strategies hardly means that we live in a 'planned economy'. Planned economies are associated with communist societies in which government agencies direct all economic activity according to their own agenda (Chang knows this, of course, and titles this chapter of his book 'Despite the fall of communism, we are still living in planned economies'). One reason why planned economies fail is that the planners have no price mechanism to inform them about supply, demand, costs and the value consumers put on goods and services. The planners lack the information to respond to changes in the market and are liable to cause widespread havoc, including famines, if they are misguided, uninformed or foolish.

It is fatuous to equate the competitive free market with its mirror image. *Of course* entrepreneurs draw up business plans, but they are privately arranged and must compete with thousands of other business plans. Their plan may fail, but unless the government foolishly bails them out, the cost of failure is borne only by the businessman, his employees and shareholders. Others will succeed at his expense.

The key distinction is that there is no grand plan subsuming individual plans. Chang's argument amounts to wordplay. He resorts to semantics because he wants to argue for a dirigiste economy and greater regulation of markets. By reminding us that capitalism is already highly regulated, Chang intends us to embrace further regulation, but this is also fallacious reasoning. Laws should be judged on their merits. The existence of the minimum wage is not an argument for implementing a maximum wage (which Chang appears to support (Chang 2010: 257)). The prohibition of slavery is not an argument for introducing tariffs. The existence of regulations does not preclude the existence of a free market and the fact that government is already active in modern economies does not justify Chang's contention that 'government needs to become bigger and more active' (Chang 2010: 260).

Conclusion

Chang is right to say that we do not live in a free market, but he is wrong about the reasons. Some regulations are necessary to underpin a free and prosperous society, but others hinder it. Supporters of a free market believe that far too many laws fall into the latter category. Many of these laws were created to serve the interests of people representing particular business interests who have no more desire to live in a free market than do socialists. 'Some restrictions on our freedom are necessary to avoid other, still worse, restrictions,' wrote Milton and Rose Friedman in 1980. 'However, we have gone far beyond that point. The urgent need today is to eliminate restrictions, not add to them' (Friedman and Friedman 1980: 69).

If supporters of a free market believed that they lived in a free market, they would protect the status quo and there would be no need for a free-market movement which aims for a more liberal economy. Although most countries have endorsed market-led reforms in recent decades, the promised land has not yet been reached. Note, however, that the promised land does not have to be reached for the benefits of particular measures such as trade liberalisation to be enjoyed. Each step along the way brings greater prosperity and liberty. This contrasts sharply with the planned economies, whose abject performance in every country that has experimented with them has been blamed on their leaders deviating from pure Marxist–Leninist theory. While left-wing critics blame the free market for every manifestation of human fallibility and greed, they permit no criticism of socialism because, they claim, a true socialist state has never existed. The only comparison they allow is between imaginary socialist utopias and existing market economies which are, more often than not, highly regulated social democracies. The French philosopher Jean-François Revel argued that the collapse of communism was a blessing in disguise for socialist intellectuals since it meant they no longer had to defend living examples of their ideology and could retreat into wishful thinking: 'Utopia is not under the slightest obligation to produce results: its sole function is to allow its devotees to condemn what exists in the name of what does not' (Revel 2009: 23).

Despite the unfortunate but indisputable fact that every attempt to create a planned economy has resulted in economic stagnation and political oppression – and that the extent of the deprivation and totalitarianism rises in direct proportion to the degree of planning – advocates of socialism contend that various degrees of central planning are desirable. Free-market economists, on the other hand, neither expect nor desire a free-for-all with no laws or regulation from any source. They only wish to see laws that promote liberty, competition, innovation and prosperity. This frequently brings them into conflict not only with socialists but with business interests and other capitalists.

Free-market economists agree that we do not live in a free market. The difference is that they would make it freer while Chang would hand still more power to the state.

PART 2

THE MYTHS

5 THE RICH GET RICHER AND THE POOR GET POORER

Belief in the systematic impoverishment of the poor is nothing new. The phrase 'the rich get richer, the poor get poorer' was referenced in the 1921 American popular song *Ain't We Got Fun?* In Britain, the same message was often repeated during the Conservative government of Margaret Thatcher. Successive Gallup surveys conducted in the 1980s found that at least two-thirds of the British public agreed with the statement 'the rich get richer, the poor get poorer'. In 1985, only 13 per cent disagreed (Heald and Wybrow 1986: 124). Today, it is not unusual to hear the same claim made by academics and journalists in various forms. For example, the sociologist Zygmunt Bauman (2005: 41) writes that 'while the poor get poorer, the very rich – those paragons of consumer virtues – get richer still'. In her best-selling book *No Logo*, Naomi Klein (2000: 122) makes the same point when she complains that the 'economic trends that have so accelerated in the past decade' have meant that 'Everybody except those in the very highest tier of the corporate elite is getting less.' More recently, the journalist Polly Toynbee asserted in *The Guardian* that the 'late 70s saw the most equal time in British history, but since then the rich have got richer and the poor poorer' (Toynbee 2012).

Sometimes the narrative of impoverishment is expanded to include not just the poor but also middle earners. In another *Guardian* article (which happened to be headlined 'On capitalism we lefties are clueless') Zoe Williams (2012) states that 'Real wages in this country have been falling since 1968'. Richard Murphy (2011: 17) is only slightly less gloomy, claiming that 'real wages for most have stagnated'. Oliver James begins his book *The Selfish Capitalist* with the unambiguous statement that 'it is a fact that one of [Thatcherism's] most significant consequences was to make the rich richer, whilst the average citizen's income did not increase at all after the 1970s. In every nation where Selfish Capitalism was introduced, the real wages of the majority either decreased or remained static' (James 2008: 2). If radio phone-ins and comments on newspaper websites are any indication, these beliefs are widely held. They are utterly and unequivocally false.

Higher wages for all

The 'poor get poorer' meme echoes the Marxist theory of 'immiseration', which predicted that the capitalist's rampant pursuit of profits would compel him to give his workers ever lower wages. In *The Communist Manifesto*, Marx and Engels wrote that 'as the repulsiveness of the work increases, the wage decreases … The modern labourer … instead of rising with the process of industry, sinks deeper and deeper below the conditions of existence of his own class. He becomes a pauper, and pauperism develops more rapidly than population and wealth' (Marx and Engels 2002: 227, 233). Some argue that Marx drew back from this theory of 'absolute immiseration' in his later work. In her history of economics, *The Grand Pursuit*, Sylvia Nasar (2012: 39) notes that a 'surprising number of scholars deny that Marx ever claimed that wages would decline over time or that they were tethered to some biological minimum. But they are overlooking what Marx said in so many words on numerous occasions.' At the very least, it is clear that Marx expected the proletariat's living standards to decline and that this would ultimately lead to revolution.

The eagerness of some Marxists to reinterpret their hero's words almost certainly stems from the fact that the immiseration theory has been soundly rebutted by history. Every capitalist country has seen a dramatic rise in real wages across every income group since Marx's day and this increase has continued during the recent period of alleged 'neo-liberalism'. Office for National Statistics data show that disposable incomes in Britain rose every year between 1970 and 2009 with the exception of the period 1973–77 and two small blips in 1980–81 and 2006–7 (Carrera and Beaumont 2010:3). By 2009, GDP had more than doubled and household disposable income was almost two-and-a-half times higher than it had been in 1970 (in real terms). Figure 2 shows that disposable incomes (solid line) in this period rose slightly faster than GDP (dotted line).

How was this income distributed? Figure 3 shows sub-stantial real-term increases for all five income quintiles between 1977 and 2011/12, with the incomes of the bottom

Figure 2 **Disposable income (solid line) and GDP (dotted line)**

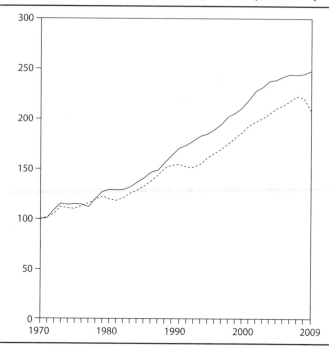

quintile rising by 93 per cent while those of the top quintile rose by 149 per cent (ONS 2013b: 10–11). Figure 4 shows thirty years of growth in disposable household income for the poorest two quintiles (in 2006/07 prices) (ONS 2012b).[1]

Even during the 1980s, when inequality rose rapidly and the number of unemployed often exceeded 3 million, the poorest quintile saw their disposable income rise in

1 The slightly different timescales in these three graphs is dictated by limitations of the Office for National Statistics source data.

Figure 3 **Real-terms increases in disposable income by quintile**

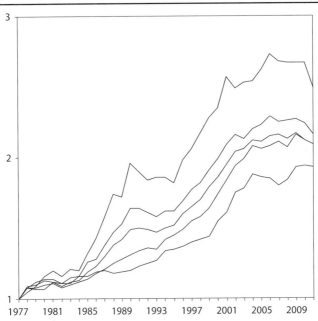

Note: 1 represents the starting point in 1977 and 2 represents a doubling in inflation-adjusted income.

real terms. By 2002/03, the bottom quintile was better paid in real terms than the second quintile had been in 1979 and the second poorest quintile was better paid than the second richest quintile had been in 1977 (ibid.). With only occasional fluctuations, every quintile has seen a substantial rise in income since the 1970s.

Changes in disposable income are influenced by changes to the tax and benefit system as well as wage increases. However, an Office for National Statistics study of earnings

Figure 4 **Disposable income growth for bottom two quintiles**

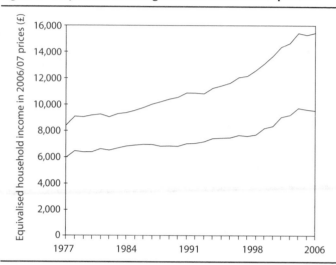

growth between 1986 and 2011 confirms that there have been significant above-inflation pay rises across the board. The data show that median earners have seen their hourly wage rise by 62 per cent since 1986, from £7.78 to £12.62 (in 2011 prices). As with disposable incomes, wage growth has been somewhat slower at the bottom of the income ladder, but hourly rates of pay have still increased significantly, rising by 49 per cent in the bottom quintile (from £4.76 to £7.08 in 2011 prices) (ONS 2012c).

Going further back, since 1975, average wages have increased by 101 per cent for full-time workers and by 87 per cent for part-time workers (87 per cent). Among the poorest decile, full-time wages rose from £3.40 to £6.67 between 1975 and 2013 (in 2013 prices) and part-time wages rose from £2.83 to £5.83; increases of 96 per cent and 106 per cent respectively. In 2013, only 2 per cent of full-time workers earned the minimum wage (£6.19 per hour) whereas 45 per cent of full-time workers earned less than this in 1975 (in 2013 prices) (ONS 2014b: 11).

The progress of the poor relative to the rich

The poor get wealthier

Discussions about 'the rich' and 'the poor' tend to focus on income rather than wealth. Wealth has always been much less evenly distributed than income. We accumulate wealth as we age, so the young often have very little if any of it. Even allowing for this, the poor have historically had virtually no assets at all and many people had debts that exceeded the value of their meagre possessions. As late as 1970, the poorest half of the British population had a 0 per cent share of the country's wealth (Dorling et al. 2007: 4). By 2010, this had risen to 14 per cent (ONS 2012d: 7). By contrast, the share of wealth held by the rich fell sharply in the twentieth century. Between 1923 and 2003, the proportion of net wealth held by the richest 1 per cent fell from 61 to 21 per cent and the share held by the richest five per cent fell from 82 to 40 per cent (Dorling et al. 2007: 4).

And some of the poor become rich

A further confusion arises from the implicit assumption that 'the rich' and 'the poor' are the same people over time. It is difficult to argue that someone who comes from a poor background and moves into the top income bracket is an example of the rich getting richer, even if that income bracket is wealthier than it used to be. As Sowell (2011: 44) notes, statistical categories should not be mistaken for flesh-and-blood human beings. The rich and the poor are not fixed groups, but individuals who move up and down the ladder over the course of their lives. Recent research from the US shows that two in five Americans will find themselves in the top 5 per cent of the income distribution at some stage of their life and nearly three-quarters will spend at least a year in the top 20 per cent (Rank 2014). As we shall see in Chapter 11, Britain is also more socially mobile than is often assumed.

And the poor get richer

These issues aside, the evidence shows that, whether measured in cash or real terms, whether looked at in terms of hourly, weekly or annual earnings, and whether taken before or after housing costs have been deducted, the last thirty years have been an era of rising prosperity across the board. These facts are so incontestable that left-wingers have had to go to great lengths to paint a picture of twenty-first century immiseration. The Trades Unions Congress (TUC), for example, uses the claim that wages have fallen *as a proportion of GDP* since the mid 1970s (from a peak of 65.5 per cent in 1975 to below 55 per cent today) as evidence that 'middle income Britain' has experienced 'shrinking wages' (Lansley 2009: 1). Leaving aside the vexed question of whether earnings have been decoupled from growth,[2] it is disingenuous to conflate a lower share of GDP with 'shrinking wages'. If 'middle-income Britain' refers to the median household, then real disposable incomes more than doubled between 1977 and 2011/12, from £11,200 to £23,200 in 2011/12 prices (ONS 2013a: 5). The Office for National Statistics notes that 'growth in UK median household disposable income since 1977 has closely mirrored growth in GDP per person, rising during periods of economic growth and falling after the recessions of the early 1980s, early 1990s and late 2000s' (ibid.).

Should we worry about relative poverty?

Critics of capitalism give the misleading impression of immiseration by referring to 'relative poverty' and income inequality as if they were proxies for real wages and living

---

2 Pessoa and Van Reenen (2013: 12) find little change in the proportion of GDP going to labour over this period, saying: 'Although there is variation over the business cycle, the share of income going to labour in 2010 was basically the same as it was 40 years ago. Indeed, there has been more of a fall in the labour share of income in continental European countries and Japan. This might be evidence of capitalists doing a lot better than workers in these countries whereas workers have done relatively better in the UK and the United States.' Wages made up an exceptionally high proportion of GDP in 1975 (the TUC's reference point) as a result of the poor state of the economy. The TUC report acknowledges that 'The "profits squeeze" which accompanied the sharp rise in wage share is now widely accepted to have been detrimental in its economic impact, contributing to inflationary pressure, a squeezing of business investment and the weakening of Britain's productivity and growth rate' (Lansley 2009:7).

standards. They are not. On the contrary, reductions in both inequality and relative poverty typically coincide with periods of general impoverishment which also hurt the poor. Between 1974 and 1976, for example, average household income was lower in real terms than it had been in 1973 and yet this period is looked on with nostalgia by those who over emphasise income equality. Polly Toynbee calls it the 'most equal time in British history' while the TUC complains that in subsequent years 'middle- and lower-income households have found themselves slipping steadily behind higher income groups in the prosperity stakes' (Lansley 2009: 6). It is true that income inequality was relatively low in the mid 1970s, but they were dark days by every other economic measure and the less-well-off made little if any progress in absolute terms.

We shall return to the issue of income inequality in Chapter 9. For now, it is sufficient to note that, while relative measures have their place, they do not tell us whether people's incomes are going up or down. The official (relative) poverty line is generally understood to be an income that is less than 60 per cent of the median.[3] To all intents and purposes, it is a measure of inequality, not of poverty. Just as changes in income inequality do not tell us whether the poor have more money to spend, a rise in relative poverty is not necessarily indicative of the poor getting poorer. In 1979, 13 per cent of the population were living below the relative poverty threshold. By 2005, the real disposable incomes of the poorest fifth had risen by more than 50 per

---

3   In 2012/13, the median weekly income was £440 and the relative poverty line was £264, or £13,766 per annum.

cent and yet 18 per cent of the population were now living in relative poverty (Adams et al. 2012: 58).[4] To put it another way, raising the incomes of Britain's poorest people by half did not prevent the official poverty rate rising by half.

Conversely, it is possible for people to be lifted out of relative poverty even as they get poorer, so long as the wages of those on median and high incomes fall even more sharply. This is precisely what happened during the recent financial crisis. In 2010/11, Britain's (relative) poverty rate fell to 16 per cent and the child poverty rate fell to 18 per cent. Both figures were lower than they had been at any time since the mid 1980s, despite – or rather *because of* – incomes falling across the board, as the Department for Work and Pensions explains (Adams et al. 2012: 23):

> Lower-income households saw smaller decreases in income, as such households are typically less dependent on earned income, with more of their income from benefits and tax credits. Benefit and tax credit income grew in cash terms and fell only slightly in real terms. This meant that households in the bottom quintile saw their income fall less in 2010/11 than households at the middle quintile, and that households at the middle quintile saw their income fall by less than households in the top quintile.

As the economy flatlined in 2012/13, several charities stopped citing relative poverty figures and began talking

---

4   Figures refer to relative poverty before housing costs. After housing costs, the figures are 13 and 22 per cent respectively (Adams et al. 2012: 58).

about absolute incomes for the first time in years (for example, Butler 2013). Relative measures had suddenly become redundant in the campaign for income redistribution. Although it had been expedient to use relative figures when the economy was flourishing, their continued use in harder economic times would have given the public the impression that things were getting better and, by implication, that the solution to poverty is recession.

Meanwhile, the government responded to the claim that 900,000 people had been 'plunged into poverty' (based on *absolute* income data) by highlighting reductions in *relative* poverty. It was further evidence that poverty can appear to be rising or falling at any given time depending on which measure is used. It also demonstrated the tendency of the two measures to move in opposite directions. When GDP is rising, absolute incomes tend to rise and relative poverty tends to rise with it. When GDP falls, average incomes tend to decline and more people are 'lifted out of poverty'. In short, the poverty rate has very little to do with how much money the poor have. The UK's official poverty rate in 2012 (16 per cent) was higher than that of Bangladesh (14 per cent), Azerbaijan (2 per cent) and Namibia (0 per cent) (Garroway and de Laiglesia 2012: 40–43).

Conclusion

Jean-Françoise Revel wrote in 1976 that 'socialists and Communists periodically announce that purchasing power continues to diminish and the workers' living conditions are steadily getting worse – which, considering their standard of living at the dawn of the industrial revolution, means the workers must by now be existing in the most abysmal misery' (Revel 1977: 154). It is unsurprising that repeated assertions of spiralling inequality and rising rates of relative poverty have given people the impression that the poor are getting poorer. As it happens, the claim that inequality and relative poverty are on the rise is not true either, but that is beside the point since neither measure tells us whether the poor are better off in any meaningful sense.

To resolve that question, we need only look at the indisputable evidence of inflation-adjusted incomes and salaries which show substantial rises across every group in Britain. It is certainly true that the rich have got richer in the period of supposed neo-liberalism, but it is emphatically not true that the poor have got poorer. Most workers in the UK say that they are 'well paid for the work they do', according to a European survey, unlike workers in such countries as Sweden, France and Finland, where this is a minority view (Kasparova et al. 2010: 10). Although the disposable incomes of the poorest households have not risen as quickly as those of the median household, the rate of growth has not been trivial. Official figures show that the disposable income of the poorest fifth of households grew by an average of 93 per cent between 1977 and 2011/12 (ONS 2013c: 10). To claim that the poor have got poorer when their incomes have nearly doubled is absurd. Revel's socialists were wrong in 1976, Marx was wrong in 1848 and the doomsayers are wrong today.

6   WE ARE WORKING EVER LONGER HOURS

'If there's one thing practically all futurologists once agreed on,' writes Owen Hatherley in *The Guardian*, 'it's that in the 21st century there would be a lot less work. What would they have thought, if they had known that in 2012, the 9–5 working day had in the UK become something more like 7am to 7pm?' (Hatherley 2012). One such 'futurologist' was the economist John Maynard Keynes, who predicted in a 1930 essay that 'the standard of life in progressive countries one hundred years hence will be between four and eight times as high as it is today' (Keynes 2009: 196). Robert and Edward Skidelsky claim that Keynes expected these new riches to come about 'because the fruits of their labour would be distributed more evenly across society' (Skidelsky and Skidelsky 2012b). Keynes did not actually say that; he said that technology would continue to increase productivity and therefore continue to increase wealth. This, admittedly, was based on the forlorn hope that there would be 'no important wars and no important increase in population' (Keynes 2009: 196), and yet he was right to believe that the 'absolute needs' of food, clothing and housing would be fulfilled for the vast majority of people in developed societies.[1] Once those needs were satisfied, he expected that 'for the first time since his creation man will be faced with his real, his permanent problem – how to use his freedom from pressing economic cares, how to occupy the leisure, which science and compound interest will have won for him, to live wisely and agreeably and well' (ibid.: 198). Assuming that people would prefer leisure to toil, Keynes expected the prosperous citizen of 2030 to work just three hours a day. The fifteen-hour week, he wrote, 'is quite enough to satisfy the old Adam in most of us!' (ibid.: 199).

It seems unlikely that Keynes's prophecy will come to pass. Indeed, there is a common perception, reflected in *The Guardian* article mentioned above, that the working day is getting longer. This is a myth that can be easily refuted with a wealth of statistics. In 1900, workers spent around 3,000 hours a year on the job. In most developed societies today, they work fewer than 1,800 hours a year (see Figure 5 – data taken from OECD (2013b)). Average annual working hours continue to decline, albeit nowhere near as quickly as Keynes predicted. Among OECD countries, average weekly hours range from 48.9 in Turkey to 30.5 in the Netherlands. In 2011, the average number of hours worked by British workers was 36.4 per week, down from 37.7 hours in 2000, which was itself less than the 38.1 hours worked in 1992. See Figure 6 (OECD 2013b; ONS 2011a).

---

1   '[A] point may soon be reached, much sooner perhaps than we are all of us aware of, when these ["absolute"] needs are satisfied in the sense that we prefer to devote our further energies to non-economic purposes' (Keynes 2009: 197).

Figure 5 **Annual working hours in the developed world, 1992–2012**

Source: OECD (2013b).

The picture is only slightly different if we look at those in full-time employment. Full-time workers in Britain put in an average of 42.6 hours per week in 2011, amounting to 8 and a half hours a day if we assume five working days per week. This is only thirteen minutes more than the EU average and it is shorter than the average working week

Figure 6   **UK average hours worked per week**

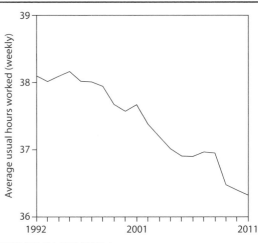

Source: OECD (2013b); ONS (2011a).

in Australia, Austria, Greece, Iceland and New Zealand, not to mention virtually all poorer countries. It is a far cry from the '7am to 7pm' shifts that some claim is the British norm and it hardly justifies *The Guardian*'s description of the UK as 'Europe's sweatshop' (Gillan 2005). In a survey of twenty countries, the British were least likely to agree with the statement 'I wish I could slow down the pace of my life' (Ipsos MORI 2013: 5).

More than half of UK workers (55.4 per cent) work less than forty hours a week (including unpaid work) (OECD 2012b). On this measure, the UK is more leisurely than both the European average (42.2 per cent) and the OECD average (36 per cent). Only 11.7 per cent of British employees work more than fifty hours a week, of whom three-quarters are men. Although this is more than the OECD average of 9.1 per cent, it is much less than countries such as Turkey (43 per cent) and Japan (29.5 per cent) (OECD 2012a). As in most wealthy countries, the proportion of Britons working these kind of hours has fallen since the mid 1990s.

Is lunch for wimps?

Overall, there is no doubt that working hours have fallen dramatically since Keynes made his prediction and they continue to fall at a slow but steady pace. The nine- to ten-fold increase in real incomes seen in industrialised countries between 1880 and 2000 coincided with a near halving of working hours (Bosch and Lehndorff 2001: 240). Moreover, the UK appears to fit comfortably within the range of comparable countries, being neither especially hard-working nor particularly leisurely. Why, then, does the opposite perception persist?

The answer may lie in changes that have occurred at the very top of the income ladder in recent decades. Although average working hours have fallen in most rich countries, the highest earners have tended to see their hours get longer while the lowest earners have seen their hours fall the most (OECD 2011: 7). Kuhn and Lozano found that longer working hours in the US are 'concentrated among highly educated, high-wage, and older men' (Kuhn and Lozano 2005: 1). Between 1979 and 2006, the proportion of American males working more than fifty hours a week increased by 11.7 percentage points in the top income quintile but fell by 8.4 percentage points in the bottom income quintile (ibid.: 6). In the EU, men are more than twice as likely to work long hours than women, and the self-employed are more than four times as likely to work long hours than employees (European Foundation for the Improvement of Living and Working Conditions 2008: 1).

Some high-fliers who work for large corporations in Britain have adopted American-style office hours as well as the attitude that 'lunch is for wimps' (another quote from the movie *Wall Street*). Those who have well-paid jobs in the City of London or work in opinion-forming occupations such as politics and journalism are likely to work much longer than average and it is their experience, rather than the lives of middle-income earners in middle England, that tends to be reflected in the national media.[2]

The implications of this new trend should not be over-looked. Historically, the poor have worked the longest hours as a matter of necessity. Today, it is the rich who tend to work longer and this, in part, explains why they are rich. Complaints about working hours today are therefore fundamentally different to those of the past. It is one thing to be concerned about millions of people having to work seventy-hour weeks in factories to put food on the

---

2 Working hours figures do not include time spent commuting to and from work, which rose between 1972 and the mid 1990s but has since fallen back to the level of the 1970s (Department for Transport 2013: 1). Workers who have long commutes earn significantly more, suggesting that they are compensated for longer journeys with higher pay. In London, for example, those who have long commutes earned an average of £18.80 an hour in 2009 while those with short commutes earned an average of £9.60 per hour (ONS 2011b: 4).

table, but quite another to worry about a relative handful of well-remunerated professionals choosing to work fifty-hour weeks in offices and boardrooms. On average, however, the facts are clear. Britons are working shorter hours than they ever have before.

Conclusion

Increased productivity has allowed average working hours to fall dramatically in every industrialised country for many decades. Where increases in productivity have slowed, the decline in working hours has also slowed. For some sections of the workforce in some countries, working hours have got longer since the 1970s, but this largely reflects these workers' preference for income over leisure.

There are two other reasons why modern society is more leisurely than is often assumed. Firstly, people are living about twenty years longer than they did in 1930, meaning that many more people are able to enjoy years of retirement; leisure therefore takes up a larger proportion of one's lifetime. Secondly, the growing availability and affordability of time-saving consumer products such as microwaves, washing machines, dishwashers and vacuum cleaners mean that fewer hours at home are consumed with domestic chores (a form of 'unpaid labour') and can therefore be devoted to leisure (Zilibotti 2007).

But the fact remains that Keynes's predicted fifteen-hour week did not come about. The reason we have not reduced our working hours to the point at which life is sustained and leisure is maximised is that once 'absolute needs' have been satisfied, most people still prefer to exchange their labour for income. If you want to work a fifteen-hour week, you can have a 1930s working-class life-style, but most people aspire to more than that, which is to say that they desire central heating, hot running water, a telephone, wall-to-wall carpets, a motor car, an indoor toilet, a computer, a television and other facilities that were either unknown or considered luxuries eighty years ago.

Nicholas Oulton (2012: 11) argues that if there had been no new inventions since 1800 we would have less to spend our money on and would therefore opt for more leisure. Everybody would have a horse-drawn carriage, but there would be 'no cars, refrigerators, washing machines or dishwaters, no radio, cinema, TV or Internet, no rail or air travel, and no modern health care' on which to spend our disposable income. Leaving aside the money we spend on taxes (which have risen enormously since 1930) and the money we spend on housing costs, most of our spending goes on products and services that were unheard of in the nineteenth century; many of which were rare or yet-to-be invented in Keynes's day.

But perhaps the simplest explanation is that Keynes ignored the possibility that 21 hours of daily leisure might be too much. 'Work–life balance' is a loaded term which implies that work is antithetical to life. This false dichotomy does not adequately reflect the fulfillment that most people get from their jobs. For many of us, work offers a blessed escape from the drudgery of family life. Countless wealthy people, including many economists, politicians and entrepreneurs, as well as musicians such as the Rolling

Stones, continue working long after they could comfortably retire. Why? Because they enjoy it.

The important question is not whether people are working the fewest possible hours, but whether their working hours reflect their true preferences. In general, the answer seems to be that they do. In their study of Australian working hours, Drago, Wooden and Black (2009: 410) found that, with a few exceptions, there was a close alignment between employees' preferred working hours and their actual working hours. The OECD found that rising working hours among sections of the US workforce 'paralleled changes in employee preferences, which have moved strongly in favour of increased earnings rather than reduced hours' (OECD 1998: 181).

When preferred working hours are not aligned with actual working hours, it is usually because workers want longer, not shorter, hours. In 2012, 4.1 per cent of the British workforce was in involuntary part-time work, which is to say that one in six part-time workers wanted to work full-time but could not. In Europe, this figure was one in five (OECD 2013a). These numbers tend to be higher when the economy is performing poorly, but there is always a significant minority of people stuck in part-time work who want longer hours.

Overall, the OECD concludes that 'in all countries, the preferences of most employees are still in favour of increased earnings, rather than reductions in hours' (OECD 1998: 154). Keynes was wrong to assume that people would prioritise leisure once the bare necessities of life are paid for.

7 RICH COUNTRIES WILL NOT BENEFIT FROM MORE ECONOMIC GROWTH

Keynes made his prediction of a fifteen-hour week in an article that was designed to counter the 'bad attack of economic pessimism' that he observed after the Wall Street Crash of 1929. 'It is common to hear people say that the epoch of enormous economic progress which characterised the nineteenth century is over,' wrote Keynes, 'that the rapid improvement in the standard of life is now going to slow down – at any rate in Great Britain; that a decline in prosperity is more likely than an improvement in the decade which lies ahead of us' (Keynes 2009: 193). Such pessimism was misplaced and the free market economies of the world continued to grow exponentially, as Revel (1977: 161) notes:

> Between 1925 and 1975 the standard of living roughly doubled (or, in some countries, tripled) despite two depressions, the first of which was truly catastrophic, despite two devastating world wars in Europe and Japan, and despite the loss of colonial empires.

Economies continued to suffer periodic setbacks, including recessions of varying magnitudes in every subsequent decade, but the march towards greater prosperity went on. Per capita GDP in the UK at the end of the twentieth century was four times higher than it had been at its start. In the USA, it was five and a half times higher. In Japan it was fourteen times higher (Hicks and Allen 1999: 23). Combined with a continuous upgrading of product quality in this period (for example, a mid-priced family car today is far superior to a mid-priced family car in 1960), this has led to a phenomenal improvement in living standards.

The economic growth experienced in the capitalist era is entirely without historical precedent. For thousands of years, the rise in global wealth was so sluggish as to be almost imperceptible. According to the economist Angus Maddison, there was a less than threefold increase in per capita incomes in the West between the years 1000 and 1820. Between 1820 and 2006, however, as countries 'acquired most of the institutional and intellectual attributes of a modern capitalist state', there was a 21-fold increase in per capita incomes (Maddison 2008: 79).

This growth has not come at the expense of poorer countries. On the contrary, when average incomes doubled worldwide between 1965 and 2000, the biggest gains were enjoyed by developing countries (Norberg 2003: 25):

> During this period, the richest fifth of the world's population increased its average income by 75 percent. For the poorest fifth of the world's population, the increase has been faster still, with average incomes more than doubling during the same period.

Figure 7 **Global real GDP per capita**

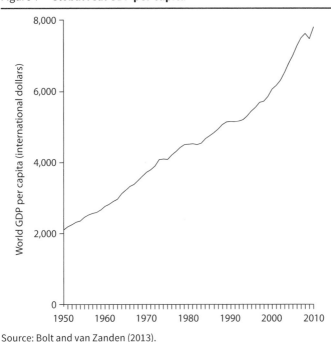

Source: Bolt and van Zanden (2013).

In total, the second half of the twentieth century saw a sixfold increase in the world's economic output (ibid.: 129). The wealth of the world's average citizen has increased by more – much more – since I was born in 1976 than it did in the entire period of history between the Trojan War and the coronation of Elizabeth II (Maddison 2008). Figure 7 shows the world's inflation-adjusted per capita GDP between 1950 and 2010 (Bolt and van Zanden 2013).

In her best-selling book *No Logo*, published in 2000, Naomi Klein (2000: 122) asserts that 'the economic trends that have so accelerated in the past decade have all been about massive redistribution and stratification of the world's resources: of jobs, goods and money. Everyone except those in the very highest tier of the corporate elite is getting less.' This is simply untrue. A study of 138 countries, representing 93 per cent of the world's population, found a 'spectacular reduction of worldwide poverty' in the last decades of the twentieth century as economies were deregulated and trade was opened up. Between 1970 and 2000, 'poverty rates declined for all conceivable poverty lines' and 'after remaining constant during the 1970s, [global] inequality declined substantially' (Sala-i-Martin 2006: 389–92). In 2010, despite the biggest financial crisis since the Great Depression, the United Nations announced that its target of halving extreme poverty between 1990 and 2015 had been met five years early.

Growth scepticism

This extraordinary success story has not killed off the pessimism Keynes identified, but today it takes a different form. The modern variety of Malthusian dread is based on the premise that the 'limits of growth' have been reached and that further growth is, at best, unnecessary and, at worst, undesirable. Prosperity itself is portrayed as the problem – the cause of 'diseases of affluence', a source of existential angst and a plague on the environment.

No one denies that economic growth has been of great benefit in the past, nor do they deny that poor countries need greater wealth today, but there are some who argue that growth should no longer be a priority because it has 'largely finished its work' (Wilkinson and Pickett 2009: 5). There is nothing original about this gloomy strand of anti-capitalism. When J. K. Galbraith made a similar argument in his 1958 book *The Affluent Society*, Harris and Seldon (1959: 62) described it as 'old hat' and accused Galbraith of regurgitating the 'musty myth of the inter-war years which proclaimed that the problem of production had been solved and that all that remained was to distribute the superabundance.'

The rise of environmentalism and the emergence of the New Left in the 1960s and 1970s saw a resurgence of 'growth sceptic' beliefs which were intertwined with concerns about population growth and inequality. When Nordhaus and Tobin wrote their influential article 'Is Growth Obsolete?' in 1972, their answer was 'not yet', but the Club of Rome's *The Limits of Growth*, published in the same year, heralded the return of Malthusian pessimism. When the New Zealand Values Party, which later became the Green Party, contested the 1972 election, it did so on a ticket of 'zero economic growth and zero population growth' (Green Party of New Zealand, n.d.).[1] They were not alone. Writing in 1980, Friedman and Friedman (1980:

---

[1] At the time, New Zealand had a population of 3 million. It has since risen by 50 per cent to 4.5 million.

1919) noted that 'whatever the announced objectives, all of the movements in the past two decades – the consumer movement, the ecology movement, the back-to-the-land movement, the hippie movement, the organic-food movement, the protect-the-wilderness movement, the zero-population-growth movement – have had one thing in common. All have been antigrowth.'

In defence of growth

The first mistake that critics of growth make is to regard the pursuit of money as a narrow goal. It is not. Whether we talk in terms of GDP, wealth or income, the pursuit of money is as broad a goal as one could wish to see. Money is, after all, only a token with which we can pursue our real goals. One might as well criticise people for 'narrowly' pursuing food, drink, shelter, education, healthcare, travel, entertainment and comfort. 'The ultimate ends of the activities of reasonable human beings are never economic', wrote Hayek. 'Strictly speaking there is no "economic motive" but only economic factors conditioning our striving for other ends. What in ordinary language is misleadingly called the "economic motive" means merely the desire for general opportunity, the desire for power to achieve unspecified ends. If we strive for money it is because it offers us the widest choice in enjoying the fruits of our efforts' (Hayek 2001: 92–93).

The second mistake is to see economic growth as a tap that can be turned on and off. Growth sceptics imagine that prosperity exists because some central power has willed it. It is true that the government can do many things to help or hinder economic progress, but growth is not the result of some grand design. It does not require any specific intent; rather it is the natural consequence of human ingenuity and ambition leading to new innovations and greater efficiency.

Few consider what it means to 'abandon the pursuit of growth' (O'Neill 2013) or '"dethrone growth" as our objective for society' (Peck 2012). It would require a conscious decision to obstruct human behaviour and throw sand in the gears of the economy. To be clear, a 'steady-state' economy is one of permanently stagnant wages. Attaining greater wealth in such a society really is a zero-sum game – you can only get richer by making someone else poorer. Adam Smith observed in *The Wealth of Nations* that wages only increase when national income increases (Smith 1957: 61–62) and we saw in Chapter 5 how closely earnings are tied to GDP.

What would have happened if we had brought economic growth to a halt in the 1970s when *The Limits of Growth* was published and people were asking whether growth was 'obsolete'? To answer that, we must remind ourselves of what life was like forty years ago. We saw in Chapter 5 that average incomes were far lower than they are today. Half of all British households did not have a telephone, half did not have central heating and a third did not have a washing machine (Sandbrook 2012a: 13). Many parts of the UK were even less affluent, as the historian Dominic Sandbrook (2011: 28 – emphasis in the original) recounts:

In Sunderland, nine out of ten families in privately owned houses had no indoor toilet, three-quarters had no bath, and half did not even have *cold* running water. As late as 1973, more than 2 million people in England and Wales lived without either an inside toilet, a bathtub or hot running water.

Few would wish to return to this standard of living, but such conditions nevertheless represented unprecedented prosperity at the time and were a vast improvement on the conditions of the 1950s (when Britons had 'never had it so good', as Harold Macmillan famously – and correctly – said). Then, as now, there were those who said that we were rich enough and all that remained was to redistribute the wealth that existed.

Equal redistribution of the wealth of the 1970s would have made a trivial difference to the lives of the poor compared to the rise in incomes that came from the economic growth that followed. And yet, in every decade since, there have been those who condemned the affluence of the age and called for an end to growth. It is over thirty years since the Friedmans made their observation about the common anti-growth thread which ran through the movements of the two previous decades. To their list, we might now add climate change activism, 'steady-state economics' and 'the new science of happiness'. Organisations with names such as the New Economics Foundation and the Institute for New Economic Thinking explicitly reject what they call 'conventional' or 'mainstream' economics and call for it to be replaced by a discipline that puts much less emphasis on self-interest and individualism, and much more emphasis on altruism and collective action. All espouse the replacement of economic growth as a societal target with non-financial goals. But which ones? Other indicators of well-being and progress already exist, such as life expectancy, adult literacy, infant mortality, disposable income and crime rates. As we saw in Chapter 3, these measures figure heavily when political decisions are made – often more heavily than concerns about GDP. Composite indicators such as the United Nations' Human Development Index and the OECD's Better Life Index also exist, but it is notable that the countries which perform best in these league tables are those with high GDP and free markets. The same is true when subjective feelings of happiness, life satisfaction and trust are measured. Any number of objective and subjective measures confirm the crucial role of economic growth in improving a whole range of outcomes.

Alternative attempts at measuring the success of a society have produced results which defy credibility. Using their own 'Measure of Domestic Progress', the New Economics Foundation concluded that Britain's happiest year was 1976, a year in which inflation ran at twenty per cent, real wages fell and the nation's economy had to be bailed out by the International Monetary Fund (NEF 2004). Dire economic circumstances may not guarantee unhappiness but, as Sandbrook notes, the New Economics Foundation 'must have been using a very peculiar index of national progress, for even at the time most people regarded 1976 as a dreadful year' (Sandbrook 2012a: xix). The same think tank's attempt to compare countries using a 'Happy Planet

Index' also produced results that can most charitably be described as counterintuitive. Billed as the 'leading global measure of sustainable well-being', the index placed Costa Rica, Vietnam and Colombia at the top of the table while Denmark, Luxembourg and the United States were ranked below Haiti, Albania, Malawi and Afghanistan.

The fact remains that GDP is the only economic indicator that predicts health, well-being, living standards and literacy to any reliable degree. Even modest economic growth radically improves living standards within a generation. Norberg (2003: 81) notes that a steady rise in GDP of three per cent each year will make 'the economy, our capital, and our incomes double every 23 years.' During the economic slump of 2008–12, it became clear that nobody really wished to return to the living standards of ten years earlier, let alone to those of the 1970s. Nobody enjoyed the 'steady-state' economy which those years of zero growth brought about. Why, if nobody is prepared to go backwards, should there be such fear of moving forward?

Conclusion

For most of recent history, the political left and right were united in seeing prosperity and plenty as desirable. The original promise of socialism was that a planned economy would produce goods and services more efficiently and in greater numbers than the free market. The Soviet leader Krushchev claimed in 1956 that communism would 'bury' capitalism by the year 2000, but by the time the Berlin Wall fell in 1989, this rosy view of collective action was impossible to maintain. It is now undeniable that free market economies produce prosperity while centrally planned economies produce shortages. Those who still oppose free markets are therefore required to be half-hearted, if not actively antagonistic, towards growth. The anti-growth movement is a remnant of the anti-capitalist left which failed to fulfil the original promise of Marxist growth and, rather than concede defeat, rubbishes the game by portraying growth as something that is not worth striving for. Their suspicion of affluence has grown stronger since it became clear that a more prosperous proletariat is less inclined to support socialist radicals, a point noted by Galbraith in the 1950s when he wrote that the 'individual whose own income is going up has no real reason to incur the opprobrium of this discussion. Why should he identify himself, even remotely, with soapbox orators, malcontents, agitators, communists, and other undesirables?' (Galbraith 1987: 73).

The truth is that every country is a developing country and there are sound reasons for the political left to shake off its Malthusian fringe and support economic growth throughout the world. Aside from the importance of creating jobs and boosting wages, it is only through growth that the state will be able to afford an increasingly burdensome welfare state and the other cherished projects of social democracy. To this we might add the need for vast sums of money to pay for an ageing society and deal with climate change.

The benefits of economic growth in the past two centuries are so astounding that capitalism's greatest critics no longer deny them. Even those who would bring about a 'steady-state economy' accept that low-income countries would benefit from more growth today, even if they are loathe to acknowledge that such growth is largely contingent on richer countries trading with them. The only question is whether further economic growth would be beneficial in wealthy countries here and now. Can the very richest countries benefit from more economic growth? By its nature, a prediction can never be made with utter certainty, but we can say that the anti-growth lobby has always been wrong in the past and there is little to suggest that they are correct today. Bryan Caplan gives us a fair assessment when he writes that: 'Past progress does not *guarantee* future progress, but it creates a strong presumption' (Caplan 2007: 48 – emphasis in the original).

8   THERE IS A PARADOX OF PROSPERITY

The academic paper that is most heavily cited by growth sceptics was written in 1974 by the economist Richard Easterlin. Titled 'Does Economic Growth Improve the Human Lot?', the study made the simple but counterintuitive observation that significant increases in GDP between 1946 and 1970 had not been accompanied by commensurate increases in life satisfaction scores. Although it was clear that richer people tended to be happier than poor people in any given society, there had been no increase in aggregate happiness over time, despite nearly everybody getting wealthier. When shown on a graph, the data from the US and some other countries, including the UK, appear to show levels of happiness – as measured by surveys asking people how happy they are – staying fairly constant while GDP surges upwards. This has become known as the Easterlin Paradox and it has been cited as proof of the futility of pursuing economic growth ever since.

The evidence for this supposed paradox remains controversial and several recent studies have contested it (Stevenson and Wolfers 2008; Deaton 2008; Veenhoven and Vergunst 2013). However, it is not necessary to debunk the evidence in order to challenge the notion that Easterlin's work shows that we need to '"dethrone growth" as our objective for society' (Peck 2012). If growth is to be dethroned then some other objective must replace it, and yet the point that is often missed about the happiness data is that if economic growth has failed to increase well-being then so has everything else. Every development of the last sixty years – the rise in life expectancy, the creation of the welfare state, the changes in the rates of crime, divorce and unemployment – has, by the logic of the 'paradox of prosperity', had no impact on levels of well-being. Those who dismiss the benefits of growth while claiming that happiness levels will be raised by reducing inequality and increasing public spending must contend with the fact that Easterlin's evidence suggests that greater government spending in recent decades has not improved well-being, nor has greater inequality reduced it.

A further point that is often overlooked is that there were no happiness surveys before the 1940s and so it is not as if well-being was rising before the post-war boom and then suddenly flat-lined. For all we know, happiness levels have been flat since Roman times. There is no way of knowing. Nor do we have a counterfactual. We do not know what would have happened to Western happiness if there had been economic stagnation or decline (although the lower happiness scores in the former USSR give us a clue). All we know is that rich countries are happier than poor countries and rich people are happier than poor people.

The obvious explanation for the supposed paradox of prosperity – which Easterlin himself gave in 1974 – is that people's happiness is relative to their aspirations and their aspirations rise in line with their standard of living. As Kahneman and Krueger (2006: 16) explain:

> If people gradually adjust their aspirations to the utility that they normally experience, an improvement of life circumstances would eventually lead them to *report* no higher life satisfaction than they did before, even if they were *experiencing* higher utility than previously. In this scenario, experienced utility could rise even while one's global evaluation of life satisfaction remained constant. [Emphasis in original]

Human beings certainly have a remarkable ability to adapt to both good and bad fortune. As an extreme example, one study showed that the life satisfaction scores of people who become severely disabled come close to returning to their pre-disability level within two years (Oswald and Powdthavee 2006). Although it is a myth that paraplegics are as happy as lottery winners, their life satisfaction levels are closer together than might be expected.[1] One such study of paraplegics and lottery winners (Brickman et al. 1978) has become a classic of the social sciences

---

1   It is also a myth that lottery winners are less happy than the general population. The evidence shows that they are typically happier or as happy as non-winners (Brickman et al. 1978; Eckblad and von der Lippe 1994; Kuhn et al. 2008). The belief that lottery winners are miserable probably stems from well-reported examples of winners who get divorced, imprisoned or are declared bankrupt. This myth consoles those who have not won. They nevertheless continue to buy tickets.

and is regularly used as a parable to discourage people from buying lottery tickets (Plumer 2012; Thompson 2012). It is, however, hard to imagine it being used to discourage people from wearing crash helmets, although that would be an equally logical lesson to draw. We would rightly view such advice as absurd and dangerous, but it is no worse than saying that economic growth should be discarded as an objective on the basis of the Easterlin Paradox.

Regardless of what happiness scores people award themselves, there are obvious, objective benefits to being a lottery winner and obvious, objective disadvantages to being severely disabled. This is quite clear from the text of the lottery winner/paraplegic study (Brickman et al. 1978: 920, 924):

> The large majority of the changes mentioned [by the lottery winners] were positive, including financial security, increased leisure time, easier retirement, and general celebrity status. Negative effects of winning, if any, were always mentioned together with some positive feature ... They rated winning very high in relation to the best thing that could possibly happen to them. They typically listed positive life changes as resulting from the windfall, such as decreased worries and increased leisure time. This suggests that winning lessened the stress and strain of their lives.

The accident victims, by contrast, 'rated themselves significantly less happy in general than the controls' (i.e.

healthy non-winners selected at random) (ibid.: 924).[2] This was hardly surprising considering their suffering (ibid.: 920):

> The life changes faced by the victims were severe and clearly evident. These formerly independent individuals now found themselves in a state [of] near physical help-lessness, in wheelchairs or beds, with their days at the rehabilitation center filled with therapy sessions.

Humanity's ability to adapt to great wealth as well as terrible hardship is remarkable, but the fact remains that the blind would rather see, the lame would rather walk and the poor would rather be rich. Our ability to shift our aspirations and adapt to new circumstances is surely the best explanation for why so many objective improvements in the post-war world have not been accompanied by dramatic improvements in our subjective well-being.

---

2   This finding is routinely misrepresented in both the popular and academic press. The average happiness score of the paraplegics was 2.96 out of five, compared with 4.0 out of five for the lottery winners. The authors argue that these scores are higher and lower (respectively) than might be expected. This is arguably true, although it is rare for people to give very high or very low scores in surveys of this kind. It is certainly not the case, as is often claimed, that the scores were virtually identical. Oswald and Powdthavee (2006) provide stronger evidence that unexpected disability does not greatly reduce life satisfaction in the long term. Smith et al. (2005) add the further observation that disabled people's well-being declines by less if they have an above-average income.

The subjective nature of self-reported happiness scores means that well-being surveys should be treated with caution. Being subjective, happiness can only be measured by asking people to report it themselves, usually by giving themselves a score out of five, seven or ten. In the view of some critics, this makes the field of happiness studies 'not even a pale imitation of proper sciences, such as physics. It is a parody of proper science' (Whyte 2013: 98). The combination of self-reporting and subjectivity certainly leaves room for scepticism, but even if the evidence was more robust, the scope for politicians to fruitfully intervene would be limited. If there is truly little difference between the happiness of a lottery winner and a paraplegic – whose circumstances are poles apart by any objective measure – then it is unlikely that a politician can do much to improve the happiness of ordinary people. But if – as common sense suggests – there is a big difference between the two, then it does not bode well for the field of happiness studies that such extremes are not apparent in the data.

Other people's consumerism

The 'new science' of happiness (Layard 2006) has led some of its proponents to demand greater state intervention to improve subjective well-being. However, the political agenda founders on the fact that much of the 'science' indicates that the factors which affect our well-being are not ones that can be easily manipulated by government. A large part of one's happiness is innate. As Kahneman and Krueger (2006: 8) note, 'measures of temperament and personality typically account for much more of the variance of reported life satisfaction than do life circumstances'. Many of the findings from 'happiness studies' are banal (e.g. 'the lowest life satisfaction is apparently experienced by those who have teenagers at home' (ibid.)) or involve factors that are beyond the state's control, such as age, a happy marriage, genetic predisposition and religious belief. Of the factors that can be tinkered with by political action, most are already government priorities – raising incomes, tackling unemployment, improving education, encouraging good health and so on.

But although the pro-state/anti-growth agenda is often advanced with reference to scientific claims about happiness and well-being, it would be wrong to assume that its proponents are wholly motivated by evidence. Robert and Edward Skidelsky, the authors of *How Much Is Enough?*, admit that their anti-growth stance does not depend on the rights and wrongs of the Easterlin paradox; rather it is based on a deeply rooted intuition about what constitutes the good life (Skidelsky and Skidelsky 2012b):

> Opposition to the growth juggernaut has gathered pace in recent years. Growth, say critics, is not only failing to make us happier; it is also environmentally disastrous. Both claims may well be true, but they fail to capture our deeper objection to endless growth, which is that it is senseless. To found our case against growth on the fact that it is damaging to happiness or the environment is to invite our opponents to show that it is not, in fact, damaging in those ways – an invitation they have been quick

to take up. The whole argument then disappears down an academic cul-de-sac. The point to keep in mind is that we know, prior to anything scientists or statisticians can tell us, that the unending pursuit of wealth is madness.

Having laid their cards on the table, the Skidelskys outline the standard anti-growth philosophy:

> The material conditions of the good life already exist, at least in the affluent parts of the world, but the blind pursuit of growth puts the good life continually out of reach. Under such circumstances, the aim of policy and other forms of collective action should be to secure an economic organisation that places the good things of life – health, respect, friendship, leisure, and so on – within reach of all. Economic growth should be accepted as a residual, not something to be aimed at.

If the Skidelskys' vision of the good life is so self-evidently correct – if the pursuit of wealth is 'madness' – it raises the question of why they need to reach for coercion. It is one thing to be disdainful of affluence and reject mass consumerism for oneself, but quite another to push one's vision of the good life onto others. Some of the popular literature on happiness economics resembles self-help books, philosophical texts which urge the reader to eschew materialism in favour of spending more time with friends or appreciating the wonders of nature. The messages of this 'voluntary simplicity' movement will seem profound or banal depending on the reader, but they have a long pedigree that reaches back to Aristotle, Buddha and Jesus. Not all happiness gurus are so benign, however. Among the coercive policies put forward in the name of well-being in recent years are higher taxes on income to discourage 'too much work' (Layard 2006: 152), food rationing (Lawson 2009: 198–200), a progressive consumption tax (Frank 1999; Skidelsky and Skidelsky 2012a) and taxing or banning advertising (Murphy 2011: 286–88; Skidelsky and Skidelsky 2012a). The implicit justification for such measures is that the guru knows better than the individual how life should be led. In the view of this elite, the masses are mistaken if they prefer income to leisure and they are deluded if they think that their quality of life will be improved by greater wealth. The Skidelskys make this quite explicit, saying that 'people should first of all get what they need, not what they want' (Skidelsky and Skidelsky 2012a: 208).

But how do they know what we need? Surely all conceptions of the good life are subjective. They depend on the preferences and circumstances of individuals who have different priorities which change over time. The preferred work–life balance of a young single person working in finance is unlikely to be the same as that of a wealthy 60-year-old grandparent. It is notable that the growth sceptic movement is dominated by affluent, left-leaning, privately educated, middle-aged males such as Robert Skidelsky, Richard Layard, Oliver James, Jonathon Porritt, Richard Wilkinson and George Monbiot. They are united by the common bond of personal wealth and some have argued that a contempt for mass consumerism lies at the heart of the anti-growth philosophy. 'Growth sceptics are in essence trying to defend their privileged lifestyles against what they see as the plague of popular consumption', writes Daniel Ben-Ami (2010: 64). This manifests itself in complaints that products are too cheap (e.g. budget airlines, Primark clothes, supermarket alcohol) or that people have too much money. They propose dealing with this perceived problem by raising prices (e.g. minimum pricing for alcohol, airline taxes, consumption taxes) or restricting incomes (by limiting economic growth), thereby preventing the lower orders from catching up with them.

The irony, as Ben-Ami notes, is that those who are most disdainful of consumerism are 'generally more obsessed with consumption than anyone else'.[3] The real complaint of the growth sceptics is not consumerism per se but other people's consumerism, especially when the products being consumed are regarded as tasteless, cheap or heavily advertised. Harris and Seldon gave short shrift to such

---

3   In her book, *The Silent Takeover*, Noreena Hertz gives the reader a glimpse of her life as an ethical consumer, which contains enough name-dropping of expensive brands to make the crassest materialist blush: 'Open my bottle of Ecover and squeeze biodegradable liquid on to yesterday's plates crusted with residues of GM-free organic pizza. Fill a cafetière with Fairtrade coffee and boil a free-range egg. Take a "not tested on animals" Lush bubble bath. Pull on my "child labour free" Reeboks, "made by 100% union labor" Levis, and "never use furs" Chloe T-shirt. Spray my hair with a Wella non-CFC canister. Read the papers and learn about the latest McDonald's boycott ... Check mail on "we put social issues first" AOL. Send off a standard form e-mail to McDonalds, protesting at their activities in Argentina. Enter the UN hunger site, click my mouse, and silently thank American Express for donating that day's bowl of rice and mealies. All the while snacking on Ben & Jerry's "we don't cut down trees in the Amazon" ice cream' (Hertz 2002: 153–54).

snobbery when discussing the wealthy intellectuals who condemned the aspirational working class in the 1950s (Harris and Seldon 1959: 62):

> These arrogant autocrats, who normally enjoy high standards of comfort themselves, indulge in lofty laments about cultural and spiritual progress lagging behind the material. They decry ambition and striving to improve one's lot in life as though it were unworthy.

The belief that other people are obsessed with material goods is not confined to intellectuals. A 1995 survey conducted by the Harwood Group found that more than 85 per cent of Americans said that their 'guiding principles' were responsibility, family life and friendship, but less than half believed that these were the guiding principles for 'most people in our society'. The majority believed that 'most Americans are more strongly guided by prosperity and wealth than they are themselves' – a mathematical impossibility (Harwood Group 1995). Similarly, a survey in Australia found that 83 per cent believed that Australians were 'too materialistic', but when another survey asked about their own circumstances, only 38 per cent said that having more money to buy things was 'very important' to them (Hamilton and Mail 2003: 3).[4]

---

4   It is interesting to note that people in the UK appear to be (or claim to be) less materialistic than citizens of most other countries. Only 16 per cent of Britons agree with the statement 'I measure success by the things I own'. This is significantly less than the world average of 34 per cent and much less than in emerging economies such as China (72 per cent) (Ipsos MORI 2013: 3).

Ferraris, Porsches and other preferences

The tendency to attribute the consumption of others to crass materialism while disowning such feelings oneself is nicely illustrated in Robert H. Frank's 1999 book *Luxury Fever*. Frank, an American economist, does not dismiss the benefits of economic growth – indeed he sees growth as 'the path toward environmental progress' – but he is a critic of conspicuous consumption. In keeping with many of the writers already mentioned, he believes that expensive goods are purchased primarily to acquire status among peers ('positional goods'). Frank also believes that status competition is a zero-sum game in which the person with the biggest house or the fanciest wristwatch wins. This being so, he proposes a 'progressive consumption tax' to bring the game to an end by limiting the spending of the super-rich (Frank 1999: 220). Under this system, people would be taxed at 20 per cent on everything they bought below a threshold of $39,999 a year, rising to 22 per cent on spending between $40,000 and $49,999 a year and moving up incrementally until the marginal tax rate is 70 per cent on spending above half a million dollars a year. His rationale is that by discouraging the consumerist arms race, people will save or invest more of their money.

The irony is that despite Frank's concerns about conspicuous consumption, he is a fan and keen purchaser of luxury sports cars. As he explains in ample detail in *Luxury Fever*, the vehicle he really wanted in the late 1980s was a Porsche 911 but he reluctantly passed up the chance to buy one at a bargain price because his 'small upstate college town has a strong, if usually unstated, social norm against conspicuous consumption ... At that time, a red Porsche convertible really would have been seen as an in-your-face car in a community like ours' (ibid.: 168). Fearful of a negative reaction, he drove a more modest vehicle around campus until the mid 1990s, when he purchased a BMW. Even then, he worried that people would assume that he had bought the car as a status symbol rather than as a speedy and reliable automobile. 'To be sure,' he writes, 'I would be more comfortable if others knew that I bought the car not to flaunt my economic good fortune but for other, more practical reasons ... the BMW accelerates more briskly, handles more surely, brakes more swiftly, and gets much better ratings in crash tests. After comparison test drives, I instantly realized that the only reason for not buying the BMW was my apprehension about what others might think' (ibid.: 203).

Compared to his British counterparts, who argue that DVD players and new sofas are unnecessary luxuries (James 2007: 237), Frank is an unlikely anti-consumerist. As an example of frivolous, uninformed and unnecessary luxury spending, he cites the Ferrari 456 GT, then on sale at $207,000, which was attracting the attention of the wealthy status seeker in the late 1990s. In Frank's opinion, it is an inferior vehicle to the Porsche 911 Turbo which costs half the price. Because the Porsche is 'even faster than the Ferrari' and 'more surefooted' (Frank 1999: 218), Frank argues that the appeal of the Ferrari lies only in its higher price and relative scarcity. In his view, those who buy it are irrational consumers flashing their wealth and making everybody else feel inadequate. Frank's progressive consumption tax is designed to deal with this kind of vulgar and wasteful consumption by deterring frivolous purchases at the top end. He envisages that a 70 per cent consumption tax will mean that 'the person who would have spent $207,000 on a Ferrari now decides to invest a little more in the stock market and spend a little less on his car. If he buys the Porsche, his outlay, including the consumption tax, will be $178,500. In return, he gets a car that performs just as well as the Ferrari and, assuming others have responded similarly, is now also just as rare' (ibid.: 218). Frank sees this as a win–win; people will save money without affecting their position in the status race. Without such a tax, however, he foresees the following outcome (ibid.: 220):

> If we continue for several more decades on our current trajectory, the replacement for today's Ferrari 456 GT will sell not for $207,000 but for more than $400,000. Those who are content to drive the $105,000 Porsche 911 Turbo today will move up to a car something like the Ferrari 456 GT. Likewise, those who drive the $72,000 Porsche Carrera today will move up to a car like the 911 Turbo. The current drivers of the $45,000 Porsche Boxster will trade up to a car like the Carrera. Today's drivers of the BMW Z3 (about $30,000) will move up to something like the Boxster. And today's entry-level sports-car drivers will move up from the Mazda Miata (about $23,000) to a car more like the Z3.

A terrifying vision of the future, indeed!

This little example illustrates three common themes in anti-consumerist literature. Firstly, that the amount of wealth and luxury that is deemed sufficient for a happy life is dictated by the personal tastes and resources of the writer. As a wealthy man with an appetite for fast cars, Frank's tastes are far from austere, but he still disapproves of what is – in his view – unnecessary consumption. Writing in the eighteenth century, Adam Smith argued that butcher's meat and linen shirts were luxuries.[5] In the 1950s, Galbraith said the same about wall-to-wall carpets, televisions and vacuum cleaners. By the 1990s, such luxuries were viewed as necessities and, according to *Luxury Fever*, the line between rational consumption and conspicuous consumption hovered somewhere between the Porsche 911 and the Ferrari 456 GT. These shifting sands are a tribute to the rapidly rising affluence of the last two hundred years and yet intellectuals continue to argue that we must now say 'enough'. Very few of them now agree with Galbraith's view that the 1950s offered a sufficient standard of living and almost none of them are prepared to sacrifice their own contemporary luxuries. With remarkable consistency, the level of wealth which is 'enough' for society is the level of wealth which they themselves enjoy. It is only those who are richer than them who have got too much money.

---

5 'It may indeed be doubted whether butcher's meat is anywhere a necessary of life' (Smith 1999: 471); 'A linen shirt, for example, is, strictly speaking, not a necessary of life. The Greeks and Romans lived, I suppose, very comfortably though they had no linen' (ibid.: 465).

Secondly, Frank believes that his own preferences are rational and evidence-based while the preferences of others are irrational and inefficient. He buys Porsches for their performance while others buy Ferraris for status. Like many of those who attack consumerism, Frank believes his own consumption to be tasteful and appropriate. It is only the mindless, competitive consumption of others that is the problem. The reason Frank's lengthy discussions about his motoring dilemmas verge on the comic is that they are so far removed from the concerns of ordinary people. Many of us see a car as a machine to get us from A to B and consider any expensive automobile to be an extravagance. Others revere a Ferrari as a thing of beauty and desire it for that reason. Frank shares neither of these views. The attributes he covets in a vehicle are speed, acceleration and handling. He can therefore justify buying BMWs and Porsches, even though they are widely seen as flashy status symbols, but dismisses as victims of the hedonic treadmill those who buy more expensive sports cars. His great fear is that people will assume that he buys expensive cars for the wrong reasons ('I would be more comfortable if others knew that I bought the car not to flaunt my economic good fortune but for other, more practical reasons'), but he is not prepared to give others the same benefit of the doubt.

Thirdly, Frank recalls the social pressure against conspicuous consumption which had hindered his spending in the past ('the only reason for not buying the BMW was my apprehension about what others might think'). He believes that this prejudice is due to his living in 'a small upstate college town', thereby implying that there are special and more sophisticated social norms in his community which do not apply to the rest of society. Just as he buys products for their inherent value while others buy them for status, his supposedly unique circumstances mean that he is under pressure not to buy flashy goods while others are under pressure to spend conspicuously. His own spending is the result of careful thought and requires courage to see it through while the spending of others is the result of status anxiety, mindless consumerism and aggressive advertising. He does not consider the possibility that people who drive Porsches and Ferraris are scoffed at as posers in most communities.

Certainly there are products which people buy, in part, because they reflect wealth and status. Adam Smith noted in *The Wealth of Nations* that for most rich people 'the chief enjoyment of riches consists in the parade of riches, which in their eye is never so complete as when they appear to possess those decisive marks of opulence which nobody can possess themselves' (Smith 1957: 157). But modern critics of growth and consumerism have a tendency to assume that almost every non-essential product is a positional good. The socialist academic Kate Pickett, for example, asserts that: 'We want bigger houses and more cars, not because we need them, but because we use them to express our status' (Russell 2010). Similarly, the Skidelskys claim that 'the bulk of household expenditure, even by the poor, is on items that are not necessary in any strictly material sense, but which serve to confer status' (Skidelsky and Skidelsky 2012a: 37). These writers have created a false dichotomy in which something is either a necessity or a status symbol. They leave no room in their analysis for products which are not required for subsistence living but which nevertheless benefit the owner in various other ways. A second car and a larger house may not be necessities (although working parents of growing families may disagree), but it does not follow that they only benefit the owner by providing status. The Skidelskys may sneer at the 'stream of useless, mind-numbing consumer goods' that people buy (ibid.: 33), but that is no less a personal opinion than Frank's view that Ferraris are over-rated.

As a Porsche 911 fanatic, Frank believes that his preferred car is the best buy and his proposed tax system seems designed to keep it – and, by association, him – at the top of the pile. But no matter how much empirical evidence he offers to support his preference for the Porsche, it remains a subjective opinion. Like the Skidelskys and the happiness gurus, he conflates his own personal desires with the wants and needs of society as a whole. It is reasonable to assume that both Richard Layard and Robert Skidelsky consider a Porsche 911 to be an extravagance. Frank would disagree. All three of them would disagree on much else. Drawing on Keynes, Skidelsky has suggested that an income of £40,000 a year is 'enough' whereas Layard, drawing on happiness surveys, suggests that the true figure is less than half of that (Skidelsky 2009; Layard 2006: 33).[6] Both men list quite different

---

6   Skidelsky's estimate of £40,000 per year indicates that, by his own reckoning, Britain needs a great deal more economic growth. In his later book, he tells us that the mean average income is £21,500.

priorities in their conception of the good life. As Jamie Whyte (2013: 118) points out, the fact that these distinguished academics cannot agree on the basics should give us pause for thought:

> Set aside for a moment the contempt the likes of Layard, [Martha] Nussbaum and Skidelsky show for the actual preferences of ordinary people. They can surely see that they disagree with each other. Lord Skidelsky can see that Lord Layard disagrees with him about what is on the list of ultimate goods that people should be coerced to pursue. Yet he does not pause to doubt the reliability of his moral intuitions. He concludes that his moral sensibilities are so exalted that even the contrary opinions of another high-minded and scholarly lord are to be dismissed as failures of moral apprehension. And vice versa. Lord Layard must think that, like the rest of us who do not rate happiness the be-all and end-all of human life, Lord Skidelsky is morally benighted. If either lord could win the day, he would tax and otherwise coerce his intellectual rivals into living according to his moral vision.

If the self-appointed arbiters of the good life cannot agree with one another, the chances of them being able to judge the wants and desires of millions of strangers are approximately zero.

In other words, even if incomes were distributed evenly, we would have barely half the optimal income.

Conclusion

Aside from the serious flaws in the evidence used in the 'science of happiness', the fundamental problem with basing policy on subjective well-being is that it is – quite obviously – subjective. One man's luxury is another man's necessity. There is much about the 'happiness' and 'well-being' movement that resembles back-to-the-land romanticism and knee-jerk anti-consumerism. The movement consists of a peculiar assortment of environmentalists, socialists, Malthusians and aristocrats who are nostalgic for pre-industrial society. In their own ways, each of them seeks to subsume the choices of the individual with their own subjective preferences. They demand coercion of the masses 'for their own good', starting with what they consider to be the horror of mass consumption.

Politically, the well-being lobby tends to be left-leaning, but it is a strange kind of leftism in which the optimism of early socialism has been replaced by pessimism about what they once saw as progress. The desire to liberate the working class has been replaced by a misanthropic view of workers as materialistic sheep. The poverty of ambition among this influential section of the left is striking. As a political stance, worrying about the ennui of the affluent and complaining that shops offer customers too much choice is a far cry from telling workers that they have nothing to lose but their chains. In contrast to the early trade unionist John Burns, who complained that 'the tragedy of the working man is the poverty of his desires' (Harris and Seldon 1959: 62), a vocal section of the modern left has made consumerism a dirty word and with it the growth, advertising and capitalism that has made the working man's desires achievable.

In any prosperous society, it is trivially true to say that people spend money on non-essential items. The wealthier the society, the more non-essential products will tend to be consumed. Capitalism's ability to satiate man's wants while creating new desires is a feature, not a bug, of the free market. In explaining his own 'paradox of prosperity', Richard Easterlin wrote in 1974 that 'economic growth does not raise a society to some ultimate state of plenty. Rather, the growth process itself engenders ever-growing wants that lead it ever onward' (Easterlin 1974: 121).

Does this onward march necessarily entail 'rampant consumerism' (Ariely 2009: 109) or the 'never ending pursuit of growth' (LaTouche 2009: 2)? Not at all. Economic growth is the result of millions of individual decisions being made every day by a free people. Those who are nostalgic for the days of thrift are free to work less, reject consumerism and pursue a life of voluntary simplicity. If certain academics believe that they earn too much – a view with which many would agree – they can get off the hedonic treadmill. The fact that so few of us have chosen to join them in abandoning affluence does not mean we have been brainwashed by advertising or enslaved by capitalism. It means only that we have different visions of the good life.

The truth is that wealth is a facilitator of the good life, not an obstacle to it. Critics of the affluent society are rarely short of money themselves and their complaints are seldom echoed by people in less fortunate positions. So long as each of us has our own vision of the good life, we should be allowed to pursue it in our own way and if that involves spending money on things that professors and baronets consider tacky or frivolous then so be it. In an open society there is room for a quasi-religious, philosophical campaign against materialism, but a voluntary simplicity movement must remain voluntary if it is not to become a tyranny.

9 INEQUALITY IS RISING IN BRITAIN

Britain is suffering from 'colossal, and still growing, inequality', according to Michael Meacher, writing in *The Guardian* (Meacher 2013). Deborah Hargreaves, director of The High Pay Centre, insists that 'Inequality has been rising rapidly in Britain for the past 30 years ... If the growth in inequality continues at its current rate, we are heading towards Victorian extremes in the next 20 years' (Hargreaves 2013). Headlines such as 'Income inequality growing faster in UK than any other rich country, says OECD' (Ramesh 2011) and 'Wage inequality rises across the UK' (King 2011) are likely to give readers the impression that we are living through a time of rising inequality.

All of these claims are misleading, at best. Those who claim that the gap between rich and poor is widening can only credibly do so if they use a timeframe that stretches back several decades. Even if we start the clock in 1985, as the OECD did in the report cited above, it is not true that the UK has seen the largest growth in inequality. A number of rich countries, including Sweden, Finland, New Zealand, Israel, the United States and Germany have seen the gap between rich and poor grow wider in the last thirty years (OECD 2011: 24). The truth is that

Figure 8   **Inequality as measured by the Gini coefficient**

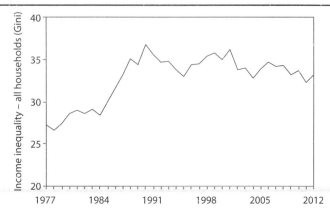

income inequality has not risen in Britain for a quarter of a century. Insofar as there has been a trend since 1990, it has been downwards.

We saw in Chapter 5 that the disposable incomes of Britain's bottom quintile rose by 93 per cent in real terms between 1977 and 2012 while the middle quintile enjoyed an increase of 109 per cent and the top quintile saw a rise by 149 per cent. This suggests that there has been a widening of the income gap, and so there has, but it was concentrated in the first 14 years of this 35 year period. There is ample evidence that inequality increased between 1977 and 1990. The top quintile increased its disposable income by 88 per cent while the bottom quintile saw an increase of only 14 per cent. However, 1990 saw the peak in inequality and the income gap has been flat or in decline ever since. Between 1990 and 2006/07, the bottom quintile increased

Figure 9 **Inequality as measured by the difference between the 90th and 10th percentile**

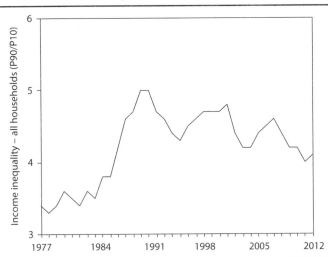

its disposable income by 40 percent, a faster rate than was seen among the top quintile, whose disposable income rose by only 29 per cent.

Figure 8 shows inequality in Britain between 1977 and 2012/13 using the standard measure of inequality, the Gini coefficient (ONS 2014a). It confirms that inequality peaked in 1990, fell during the subsequent recession and has declined somewhat in the years since, albeit with fluctuations. This finding remains true whether one looks at disposable household income (shown in Figure 8), retired households, non-retired households or the difference between the income of the tenth and ninetieth percentiles (the P90/P10 measure – see Figure 9 (ibid.)).

Why inequality rose in the 1980s

There are many reasons for the surge in inequality in Britain and elsewhere during the 1980s. In the context of this chapter, it is a pertinent fact that Geoffrey Howe, Margaret Thatcher's first Chancellor, took the decision early in the decade to tie increases in welfare payments to the rate of inflation rather than to wages. As a result, pensioners in particular did not see their incomes rise as quickly as those who were in full-time work. Moreover, the rise in unemployment in the early to mid 1980s meant that more people were reliant on unemployment benefit than before.

Speaking more generally, drivers of income inequality include technological progress that disproportionately benefits highly skilled workers; globalisation opening up markets for a few players who may get super-rich[1]; the rise in the number of pensioners, who tend to have lower incomes[2]; reductions in the top rate of income tax; 'audience magnification' allowing winner-takes-all markets[3]; and wealthy people working longer hours.

---

1   It is worth noting that globalisation has provided opportunities for some people to get very rich and has increased inequality in some countries. However, this process has also led to an unprecedented fall in global poverty.

2   Retired people typically earn between 60 and 68 per cent of their working counterparts (ONS 2008: Figure 12) though their spending needs may also be lower.

3   As an example, Robert H. Frank (1999: 38) notes that Iowa had 1,300 opera houses at the start of the twentieth century and 'thousands of tenors earned adequate, if modest, livings performing before live

Taxes, benefits and inequality

An important counterweight to these inequality-boosting pressures is the income tax and benefits system which, in the UK, is highly progressive and redistributive. Before tax and benefits, the richest fifth of households earned an average of £78,300 in 2011/12 while the poorest fifth – few of whom are in full-time work – earned just £5,400. This is a 14 to 1 ratio, but the income of households in the poorest quintile is then topped up with an average of £7,400 in cash benefits. Households in the second lowest quintile receive an average of £8,400 in cash benefits (the counter-intuitive finding of the second poorest quintile receiving more in benefits than the poorest quintile is due to more retired people being in the former group). Even those in the middle quintile – which includes those on a median income – are net recipients of state benefits on average. Once wealth has been redistributed through cash payments and benefits in kind, the 14 to 1 ratio is reduced to 4 to 1 (£57,300 and £15,800) (ONS 2013a). This is almost exactly the same ratio as in 1987. One can argue about whether this distribution

audiences. Now that most music we listen to is pre-recorded, however, the world's best tenor can be literally everywhere at once.' As a result, he says, 'Pavarotti earns several million dollars a year even as most other tenors, many of them nearly as talented, struggle to get by.' The existence of very wealthy superstars has a non-trivial effect on inequality. *The Economist* notes that 'truly global celebrities are few in number. But they have a penumbra of agents, lawyers and image-makers. As Lionel Robbins, a British economist, once said, "a substantial proportion of the high incomes of the rich are due to the existence of other rich people"' (*The Economist* 2011).

is 'fair', but it is wrong to suggest that Britain is a country in which inequality is spiralling out of control.

Inequality and recession

In 2011/12, income inequality in Britain fell to its lowest level since 1986. This came as a shock to pundits who had predicted that the combination of recession and budget cuts would make the gap between rich and poor wider. In 2009, for example, Madeleine Bunting told *Guardian* readers that 'The recession is likely to significantly deepen inequality' (Bunting 2009). Unlike many other commentators on the left, Bunting acknowledged that inequality had not risen in the previous decade, but she claimed that the economic slowdown would lead to a surge:

> The really disturbing possibility is that this recession could wipe out all of Labour's meagre achievement on inequality over the last 12 years. Their record was never very impressive, but they had managed to make some small inroads. That could all be cancelled in the next 18 months.

These fears never materialised. Instead, 2010/11 saw 'the largest one-year fall in income inequality in nearly 50 years' (Flanders 2012) and when the Office for National Statistics announced in 2013 that income inequality and relative poverty had fallen to their lowest level since the mid 1980s it was time for the left-wing press to face reality. Writing for *The Independent*, David Blanchflower said,

'Rather surprisingly inequality was substantially lower in 2011–12 than it was before the recession' (Blanchflower 2013). But this was no surprise to those who remembered previous recessions. If Blanchflower had searched through back issues of his own newspaper he would have found articles from the mid 1990s with headlines such as 'Recession narrows the gap between wealthy and poor' (Chote 1994).

Income inequality declines during recessions for the same reason that its close cousin relative poverty declines (see Chapter 5). Margaret Thatcher's decision to tie benefits to inflation was one factor in the rise of inequality in the 1980s, but it also helped to reduce inequality in subsequent recessions. As inflation rises and the demand for labour falls, workers see their incomes decline in real terms while those who rely on benefits and tax credits experience little or no reduction. Between 2007 and 2012, the top 10 per cent of earners saw their real incomes fall by the largest amount (6.3 per cent) while the bottom 10 per cent was the only group to see a real-terms increase (of 1.2 per cent) (Simon 2013).

Contrary to received wisdom, the recession hit the rich harder than the poor – if by 'hit' we mean 'reduced the income of'. In 2010/11, for example, 'real incomes fell by 1.1% at the 10th percentile, 3.1% at the median and 5.1% at the 90th percentile. The largest falls in income took place at the very top of the income distribution, with income at the 99th percentile falling by 15%' (Cribb et al. 2012: 29).

According to the Office for National Statistics (2013a: 11), low-income households were not merely cushioned from the decline in wages in the Great Recession, but actually became less poor in real terms:

> The largest fall in incomes over this period [2007/08 to 2011/12] has been for the richest fifth of households, whose disposable income has fallen by £4,200 (or 6.8%) in real terms. This has been largely driven by a fall in average income from employment (including self-employment). The average income of the middle fifth of households fell by £760 (or 3.1%) over this same period. By contrast, the average income of the poorest fifth has risen by £700 (or 6.9%) since 2007/08. This is mainly due to an increase in the average income from employment for this group, along with an increase in the average amount received in certain cash benefits such as tax credits and housing benefit.

The combination of rising incomes at the bottom and falling incomes at the top naturally led to a reduction in inequality. Similarly, when rates of inequality fell in the 1990s it was not because the disposable incomes of the poor rose, but because the incomes of the top quintile fell in 1991 and remained lower than the 1990 peak for the next six years.

Inflation-adjusted benefits and tax credits give people on low incomes a measure of protection from rising prices and falling wages which means that they are less affected by economic crises than those on median and high incomes. This can be illustrated by the differences between the incomes of pensioners and working people during the

Figure 10 **Incomes of retired and non-retired households**

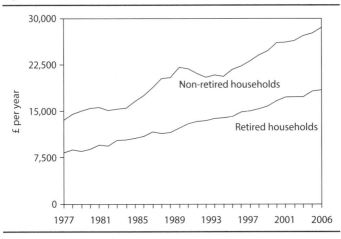

recession of the early 1990s (see Figure 10). While working households saw a prolonged slump in their earnings in the first half of the decade, the incomes of the retired continued to rise at a steady rate (ONS 2012d).

All this runs contrary to the conventional wisdom, but it is confirmed by the Office for National Statistics, which notes (Jones et al. 2008: 22):

> The Gini coefficient [of inequality] increased more rapidly during periods of faster growth in income from employment (the late 1980s and late 1990s) and either increased more slowly, or fell, during periods of slower growth in employment income (the early 1980s and early 1990s) ... in periods of rapid growth in employment income, these households 'pull away', while during periods of low or

129

falling employment income other households, those predominantly reliant on benefit and pension income, have a chance to 'catch up'.

The experience in Britain in the last hundred years indicates that growth goes hand in hand with inequality while egalitarianism goes hand in hand with economic stagnation and decline. The periods when income inequality declined – the Great Recession, the recessions of the early 1990s, early 1980s and mid 1970s, as well as both world wars – were periods of general impoverishment. By contrast, every income group does better when the economy is growing.

We shall see in the following chapter that there are some who believe that reducing income inequality is more important than generating growth. For now, we shall only note that growth and reducing inequality seem to be largely incompatible. In the modern welfare state of the UK, significant reductions in inequality have only come about as a result of economic malaise. But even if we ignore periods of recession, it is still clear that inequality has not risen since 1990.

The one per cent

We have seen that, while it is technically true to say that 'UK income inequality has soared since 1975' (Cooper 2011), this refers to a surge in inequality that took place a generation ago. This is arguably misleading, but it is simply untrue to say that 'inequality *is* rising' and it is quite ludicrous to say that 'inequality is rising more quickly than in the 1980s' (Merrick 2013).

There is, however, one measure of inequality which has risen since the early 1990s and it might explain why so much attention is devoted to the topic in political and media circles. Although less commonly used than the Gini coefficient and the P90/P10 measure, figures showing the proportion of income earned by the top one per cent indicate that the richest percentile has taken an increasingly large proportion of the nation's pre-tax income, rising from around 10 per cent in 1990 to 15 per cent in 2010 (Piketty and Saez 2012). Much of this change has been driven not just by the top one per cent, but by the top 0.1 per cent. The Institute of Fiscal Studies notes that between 1990 and 2010, 'income inequality at the very top of income distribution (comparing the 99th to the 90th percentile) continued to rise' and that 'within the top 1%, the incomes of the richest had grown fastest, with income growth at the 99.9th percentile even higher than at the 99th' (Cribb 2013: 2).

As we have seen, large rises in income among this small fraction of the population have not resulted in rising inequality in general. The gap between the relatively rich (the 90th percentile) and the relatively poor (the 10th percentile) actually declined between 1990 and 2010. To a large extent, then, concerns about rising inequality reflect changes in income distribution at the very top of the ladder. Indeed, as Richard Reeves (2013) notes, it is primarily about changes *within* the top one per cent:

I have lost count of the number of arguments I have had with rich people about the injustices of inequality – but not over the gap between their own position and that of the less fortunate 99%. No, what makes them really angry is the gap between themselves and those making more money than them within the top 1% ... Income inequality within the bottom 99% has been remarkably steady for the last couple of decades. And the gap between the bottom and the middle (i.e. the 10th and 50th percentile) has narrowed somewhat. But it is not clear that the real problem in society is the gap between the person on the 99th percentile of the income distribution, and the person on 99.6.

For those at the very top of the income ladder, the last twenty-five years may indeed feel like an era of growing inequality. As the top one per cent drifts away from the rest of the top 10 per cent, wealthy people in the professions, arts and academia see their peers and old school friends make ever-larger fortunes in finance and show business. The nouveau riche has barged past the natural aristocracy and global celebrities have raced ahead of the upper-middle classes. In his book *Richistan*, Robert Frank (not to be confused with Robert H. Frank) found a well of resentment between the haves and the 'have-yachts', with CEOs expressing bitterness towards superstar celebrities while millionaires vent their envy of billionaires. Oliver James painted a similar picture of jealousy and angst within the wealthiest classes in his book *Affluenza*.

We can only speculate about the extent to which growing inequality between the highest earners – a class that includes many public intellectuals, politicians, broadcasters and academics – has moulded public opinion about inequality, but it is notable that the resentment of the rich towards the super-rich does not seem to be widely shared by the general population. In 2007, the Institute for Social and Economic Research sought an answer to the question of why 'most people appear to accept widespread social and economic inequalities' and found that Britons were not greatly troubled by other people earning large incomes (Pahl et al. 2007):

> We find that, in many ways, social comparisons are still narrow and knowledge of the true extent of inequality is still limited. What comparisons people do make appear to be based on lifestyle and consumption. Hence, they are neither resentful of the super-rich, nor of others closer to themselves who have done better in life. However, they are very aware of their advantages compared with less fortunate members of society.[4]

J. K. Galbraith wrote in 1958 that 'Envy almost certainly operates efficiently only in regards near neighbours. It's

---

4   A study by the Work Foundation found that many people who stated concerns about inequality were actually expressing concerns about poverty; an understandable confusion since the two are often conflated by journalists, politicians and social reformers (Lee et al. 2013: 4).

not directed toward the distant rich' (Galbraith 1987: 72). Similarly, the philosopher Alain de Botton (2004: 47) notes that 'We envy only those whom we feel ourselves to be like; we envy only members of our reference group.' Empirical research supports these observations (Snowdon 2012), but in recent years a new hypothesis has been put forward suggesting that inequality has a more insidious and corrosive effect on society. It is to this theory that we now turn.

10 INEQUALITY IS THE CAUSE OF HEALTH AND SOCIAL PROBLEMS

In their bestselling book *The Spirit Level* (2009), the sociologist Richard Wilkinson and the epidemiologist Kate Pickett use international statistics to argue that 'more equal societies almost always do better'. The 'societies' in question are a selection of wealthy countries; the equality is income equality. A series of scatter-graphs show how these countries (and US states) compare on a variety of criteria when mapped against inequality. As promised by the book's subtitle, 'Why More Equal Societies Almost Always Do Better', the places with the narrowest gap between rich and poor often appear to do better. The authors insist that this phenomenon is not due to poverty, but is the result of the 'psychosocial' stress of living in an 'unfair' economy. Inequality, they say, acts like a 'pollutant spread throughout society' with rich and poor equally susceptible to its toxic effects. The lesson is clear – if you want to mend the broken society, reject 'free-market fundamentalism'.

Wilkinson and Pickett's hypothesis struck some commentators as being 'intuitively' correct. Reviewing the book in the *Sunday Times*, John Carey said that it 'formulates what everyone has always felt' (Carey 2009). Its authors do not disagree, saying that their evidence 'turns what were purely personal intuitions into publicly demonstrable facts'. Moreover, they believe that these 'facts' should 'substantially increase the confidence of those who have always shared these values and encourage them to take action' (Wilkinson and Pickett 2010a: 247).

With evidence fitting intuition so perfectly, a sceptic might suspect that confirmation bias is at work. Certainly there are many aspects of the evidence presented in *The Spirit Level* that demand a heavy dose of scepticism. Wilkinson and Pickett never acknowledge how controversial their theory is, nor do they cite the large body of literature that conflicts with it; they frequently treat poverty, inequality, class and caste as if they were interchangeable; they draw bold conclusions from ambiguous and partial evidence; they cite studies as supporting evidence despite these studies contradicting them and do likewise when quoting scholars and historical figures; they chop and change between no fewer than six different measures of inequality in the course of the book; they fail to test for statistical outliers; they rely on implausible mechanisms to explain how one economic variable can affect so many different outcomes; they make predictions that cannot be justified even on their own terms; they arbitrarily exclude several countries from their analysis; they compare datasets which, by their own admission, are not comparable; they ignore obvious third variables; they present blips as trends; they present untested assumptions as fact; they dismiss ethnic and cultural differences as irrelevant; they make naive assumptions about prehistorical human society; they apply findings of dubious relevance from animal studies to human behaviour; they use old data when newer data are less favourable to their argument, and they strongly imply that statistical significance is evidence of causation.

This chapter will restrict itself to examining just a few of the flaws in *The Spirit Level*.

Selection bias

Although *The Spirit Level* makes the striking claim that 'more equal societies almost always do better', its analysis is limited to comparing 22 rich countries, with a 23rd (Singapore) occasionally added in. In some instances, they look at only a dozen nations. Wilkinson and Pickett's justification for excluding 90 per cent of the world's countries is that inequality has the greatest impact in places which have 'reached a threshold of material living standards after which the benefits of further economic growth are less substantial' (Wilkinson and Pickett 2009: 10). Echoing the 'end of growth' arguments discussed in Chapter 7, they claim that the 'levelling off' of happiness scores in rich countries (see Figure 11) is mirrored by a flattening out of life expectancy once countries reach a certain level of wealth.[1] Two graphs show happiness and life expectancy matched against national income. Each suggests that

---

1   Life expectancy continues to rise in nearly all countries, so it is the curve that flattens off rather than the rates. This contrasts with happiness, which, according to Easterlin, has remained flat in absolute terms.

Figure 11 **Gross national income and self-reported happiness**

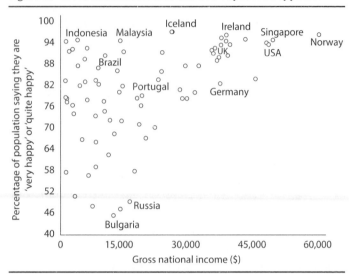

rising GDP has a dramatic effect on both variables in the early stages of development but produce diminishing returns as countries become richer.

Having made the argument that economic growth does not make rich countries happier or healthier, Wilkinson and Pickett spend the rest of the book arguing that reducing income inequality is the key to improving these, and other, outcomes. Since they do not dispute the fact that economic growth is crucial in tackling health and social problems in poorer countries, they confine their analysis to developed nations. This is not an unreasonable approach given their set of assumptions; the problem is that they select these countries in an arbitrary and unsatisfactory way. Rather than determine scientifically which countries are lucky enough to yield no further benefits from economic growth, they simply pick the fifty richest countries, as measured by the World Bank in 2002, and remove those that do not have data on inequality or have a population of less than three million (the latter rule is designed, they say, to exclude tax havens).

Why pick the richest fifty rather than the richest forty or sixty? There appears to be no rationale, fifty is simply a round number. Most of those fifty are then discarded, leaving a relatively small number of countries in the analysis. Wilkinson and Pickett justify their methods by saying that their 23 countries 'are on the flat part of the curve' in their graph showing national income and life expectancy (Wilkinson and Pickett 2010a: 280). Indeed they are, but so are several other countries that are excluded. Relatively poor (and unequal) Portugal is on their list, but countries of comparable or greater wealth – notably the Czech Republic, Slovenia,[2] Hong Kong and South Korea – are not. When these countries are added, many of the statistical relationships in *The Spirit Level* disappear. Singapore and Hong Kong happen to be the most unequal countries in the rich world and so their solid performance under most

---

2 Technically, Slovenia is excluded because it has a population of under three million, but this cut-off point is entirely arbitrary and there is no reason to ignore a country that is clearly not a tax haven. Slovenia was included in some of Wilkinson and Pickett's earlier research when their cut-off point was two million. It is puzzling that they raised it to three million for *The Spirit Level*; doing so did not exclude any more tax havens.

Figure 12 **Inequality and life expectancy (*Spirit Level* countries)**

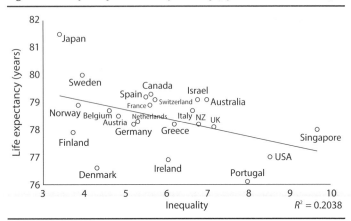

$R^2 = 0.2038$

of Wilkinson and Pickett's criteria undermines their hypothesis. The casual reader of *The Spirit Level* is unlikely to notice that Singapore is excluded from many of the graphs and that Hong Kong is excluded entirely.

The importance of country selection can be illustrated by the graph Wilkinson and Pickett use to show that income inequality leads to lower life expectancy, reproduced in Figure 12. There is a modest negative relationship between the two variables, but when the other wealthy countries are included in the analysis (Figure 13), this association is shown to be an artifact of the limited sample group. Both graphs use data from the 2004 United Nations Human Development Report, which was already out of date when Wilkinson and Pickett used it. More recent life expectancy figures have further weakened the claim that greater income inequality is associated with lower life

Figure 13 **Inequality and life expectancy (with missing countries included)**

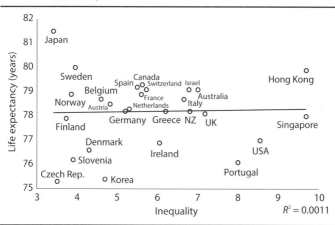

expectancy. Figures from the 2013 Human Development Report confirm that no such relationship exists, even if the analysis is confined to Wilkinson and Pickett's 23 countries.

Richard Wilkinson's inequality research had been criticised for 'cherry-picking' countries long before *The Spirit Level* was published (Lynch et al. 2000; Mackenbach 2002) and a large part of the evidence put forward in the book can be explained by this alone. The graphs showing international differences in life expectancy, trust, infant mortality, obesity, working hours, mental illness, teen births, murder and educational achievement all fall apart when the handful of countries that were excluded are put back in. This is partly because many of their correlations are so shaky that it only takes a few extra data points to shatter the illusion. As John Kay notes, 'If you remove the bold lines from the diagram[s], the pattern of points mostly looks random, and the data dominated by a few outliers' (Kay 2009). If the inequality hypothesis was more robust, the addition of extra countries would strengthen, not weaken, the statistical relationships. As it happens, however, the 'more equal' countries that were excluded tend to perform quite badly on most criteria while the 'less equal' countries of Singapore and Hong Kong tend to perform well. Without a sound reason to exclude these countries, the graphs with the larger sample size provide a better guide than those with the smaller sample.

Ignoring outliers

In Wilkinson and Pickett's life expectancy graph, Japan comes top by some distance and since Japan is the most equal country in their list, this result supports their hypothesis. But the second most equal country (Finland) comes well below average and egalitarian Denmark ranks very low. In *The Spirit Level* it is common to see most of the European countries bunched together, as they are in Figure 12, with a few countries on either extreme dictating the regression line. In this instance, the apparent correlation between inequality and life expectancy is largely the result of the Japanese's famous longevity and the relatively low life expectancy of the poorest country in the group, Portugal. By including the missing countries we can see that the slim correlation in *The Spirit Level* is the result of

Figure 14 **Inequality and homicides per 100,000**

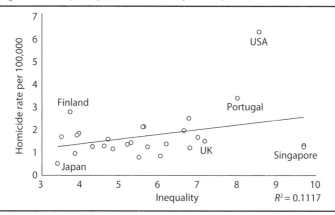

selection bias, but even if it were not, it appears that Japan is something of an outlier (Figure 13).

Several graphs in the book rely heavily on outliers, often Japan and the US. For example, Wilkinson and Pickett's claim that less equal countries have higher rates of obesity hinges entirely on the Japanese being slim and Americans being fat. This is not a novel observation, nor is it news that the Japanese have an unusually high life expectancy. Wilkinson and Pickett's claim that income inequality is the root cause of obesity rests only on these two countries being at opposite ends of their inequality scale. This requires them to overlook the fact that Singapore and Hong Kong, which are even less equal than the US, have similar rates of obesity to Japan. They must also overlook the fact that there is no correlation between inequality and obesity among the other 21 countries in their list.

It is well known that the US has unusually high rates of homicide, obesity and imprisonment. In *The Spirit Level*, this is taken as evidence that inequality lies at the heart of these issues, but if we look at all the rich countries, it is clear that the US is an outlier. There are many reasons why America has such a high homicide rate, but if inequality was one of them, we would expect countries like Britain and Singapore to have a comparably high murder rate. As Figure 14 shows, they do not. The correlation between inequality and homicide in this graph is not statistically significant (meaning that there is no correlation in statistical terms) and the only reason that the line is not completely flat is that it is being pulled up by a single outlier.

Wilkinson and Pickett make much out of their claim that there are higher levels of trust in more equal societies. Figure 15 shows the percentage of people in each country who say that 'most people can be trusted' in the World Values Survey. Because Wilkinson and Pickett exclude several countries and use old data for some of those that they do include, the graph in *The Spirit Level* shows a stronger association than actually exists, but even that correlation is driven by the unusually high trust scores of the Scandinavian countries. There is no correlation whatsoever among the rest of the countries, with unequal societies such as the US and New Zealand outperforming the two most equal societies, Japan and the Czech Republic. In truth, the only thing we can tell from Figure 15 is that Scandinavians are more trusting than people in other wealthy nations. Whatever the reason for this, the position of the other countries does not support the hypothesis that the difference is

Figure 15 **Inequality and self-reported trust**

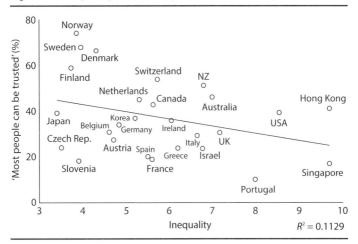

$R^2 = 0.1129$

driven by income inequality. There is no pattern among them whatsoever.

Statements such as 'America has a high murder rate' or 'Scandinavians are more trusting' are not as interesting as the claim that inequality erodes trust and causes people to murder one another. Nevertheless, such unsensational observations are all that can be reasonably derived from the data.

Dismissal of economic growth as a factor

Wilkinson and Pickett begin *The Spirit Level* by dismissing the importance of economic growth in wealthy societies on the basis that life expectancy does not correlate with GDP in the very richest countries. They are right about that, but

Figure 16 **Gross national income and self-reported happiness**

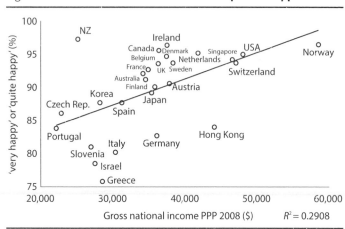

they do not test their other criteria to see whether national income plays a part. Often it does. For example, there is a stronger link between trust and GDP than there is between trust and inequality, but this relationship is never tested in *The Spirit Level*. Although they show a graph similar to Figure 11 to support their claim that 'happiness levels fail to rise further as rich countries get still richer' (Wilkinson and Pickett 2009: 8), they never check whether this is true among their group of rich countries. There is actually a positive and statistically significant relationship between GDP and happiness (shown in Figure 16) and – crucially, but also overlooked in *The Spirit Level* – there is no association between inequality and happiness.

Wilkinson and Pickett claim that economic growth 'has largely finished its work' and that the differences between rich countries must therefore be the result of some other factor, but this is little more than an assertion (ibid.: 5). Their richest country, Norway, is nearly three times wealthier than Portugal. It would be remarkable if Norway did not perform better across some criteria for this reason alone (Wilkinson and Pickett do not comment on the fact that Portugal comes bottom in both their trust and life expectancy graphs). Sure enough, the richer countries often do perform better, but this is not acknowledged in *The Spirit Level*.

Wealth plays a bigger role than the authors let on. This is particularly true of their analysis of US states, which they use as supporting evidence. As with the international evidence, Wilkinson and Pickett give short shrift to the idea that outcomes could be improved by making everybody wealthier, but when they briefly mention this possibility in regard to US states they present a graph which, they say, 'shows no clear relation between [their index of health and social problems] and average income levels' (ibid.: 21). In fact, the graph shows something very important – all of the states that are rich perform well and all of the states that perform worst are poor. This crucial fact is entirely ignored in their discussion of the numerous graphs that follow, many of which show particularly weak correlations. They never remark on the fact that the states that almost invariably perform worst – notably Missouri, Louisiana and Alabama – are not just very unequal but also very poor. Nor do they comment on the fact that very unequal but wealthy states – notably New York and Connecticut – are never among the worst performers and frequently perform rather well. Contrary to the blithe assertions of *The Spirit*

Level's opening chapter, economic growth and absolute wealth remain highly important.

Ignoring history

If inequality was a key driver of health and social problems we would expect these problems to get better or worse as inequality goes up or down. Wilkinson and Pickett make some extraordinary predictions about what would happen to infant mortality, life expectancy and murder rates if inequality in the UK fell to Scandinavian levels ('everyone would get an additional year of life, teenage births could fall to one-third of what they are now, homicide rates could fall by 75 per cent ...' and so on (ibid.: 261)). Given that they believe that there is a direct, causal relationship between income inequality and these social ills, it is surprising that they spend so little time demonstrating that relationship based on recent history. After all, we have plenty of detailed crime and health statistics, and we know how inequality has changed over the years. If society's problems rise and fall in tandem with inequality, it should be easy to prove.

In fact, there is vanishingly little evidence of any such link. Life expectancy has been rising at a similar rate through-out the Western world for decades. Crime peaked in many countries in the early 1990s and has since fallen sharply, for reasons that remain something of a mystery. Infant mortal-ity rates reach record lows on an almost annual basis. Rates of pregnancy, smoking and drug use among teenagers have fallen rapidly in the last fifteen years.

None of this has coincided with a major drop in inequality. Indeed, inequality has continued to rise in the US and in many other countries (although not, as we saw in the last chapter, in the UK). Things are manifestly not getting worse in the 'less equal' countries, nor are the 'more equal' nations racing ahead. In *The Spirit Level*'s life expectancy graph, Sweden comes second only to Japan, but in the few short years since those data were collated, less egalitarian nations, including Switzerland, Israel, Australia and Italy have overtaken it (UN 2013: 144).

In the US, the murder rate was 9.8 per 100,000 in 1991. By 2005, after years of rising inequality, it had fallen to 5.5 per 100,000 and – despite Wilkinson and Pickett's attempt to shore up their hypothesis by claiming that homicides 'started to rise again' – it has since fallen to 4.7 per 100,000 (Wilkinson and Pickett 2009: 142; FBI 2013). The same can be said for many of the problems that *The Spirit Level* claims are caused by inequality, including infant mortality and teen births. The latter has 'reached historic lows for all age and ethnic groups' (Centers for Disease Control 2012) in the US despite Wilkinson and Pickett's insistence that there is a 'reasonable match between recent trends in homicides, teenage births and inequality' (Wilkinson and Pickett 2009: 142).

None of the evidence from recent history indicates that inequality is linked to any of the problems Wilkinson and Pickett focus on. The prevalence of these problems rarely follows trends in inequality; on the contrary, it frequently travels in the opposite direction.

Mechanisms

Further questions arise when we consider how inequality could drive so many different health and social problems in practice. What is the mechanism by which income disparities lead to unfavourable outcomes? Wilkinson and Pickett argue that less equal societies are more hierarchical (ibid.: 27) and that differences in social class lead to feelings of inferiority and exclusion which manifest themselves in weakened communities, greater violence and a lack of trust (ibid.: 45). They claim that income inequality has profound 'psychosocial' effects on the population which have an impact on almost every part of life. 'Shame and humiliation', they write, 'become more sensitive issues in more hierarchical societies: status becomes more important, status competition increases and more people are deprived of access to markers of status and social success' (ibid.: 141).

This is not consistent with research that shows that people are unaware of the extent of income inequality where they live and are often indifferent to it in any case (Alesina et al. 2004; Pahl et al. 2007; Kuziemko et al. 2013). Moreover, the connection between inequality and hierarchy is another assertion by the authors, not an established fact. Early in the book, Wilkinson and Pickett say that 'it is reasonable to assume' that income inequality is a measure of how hierarchical a society is (ibid.: 27), but this is simply not true. On the contrary, the most equal society in their list – Japan – is by far the most class-bound, deferential and openly hierarchical while Australia, for example, is a largely classless society despite higher levels of income inequality. As Peter Saunders (2010a: 119) notes, Wilkinson and Pickett 'believe that income inequality causes social problems because of the psychological stress that hierarchy creates for individuals. But if this were true, Japan should appear at the opposite end of every one of their graphs, for while its income distribution might be compressed, its status antennae are as finely-tuned as in any society on Earth.' Small income differentials do not necessarily indicate an egalitarian ethos.

Wilkinson and Pickett insist that income inequality leads to psychological stress and that psychological stress leads to illness, violence, overeating and so on. Richard Smith (2011: 640) summarises their theory as follows: 'Unequal income leads to unequal status, and in a world where people are alert to and anxious about where they are positioned on the social ladder, this anxiety affects both mental and physical health. Psychological insecurity and distress rise; self-esteem falls'. The trouble with this theory is that the evidence suggests that people's self-esteem has been rising, not falling, for decades. Wilkinson and Pickett acknowledge this and try to get around it by arguing that the self-esteem measured in surveys is really a sort of quasi-self-esteem, which reflects the way schoolchildren are taught to have excessive faith in themselves, leading to narcissism. There is, they say, good self-esteem and bad self-esteem, and this is the latter. However, as Smith says, 'this looks like a rather desperate strategy on Wilkinson and Pickett's part to save the explanation in terms of concern for status and self-esteem' (ibid.: 641). Moreover, the tendency of more equal countries to have higher suicide rates does not immediately suggest that their citizens enjoy less anxiety.[3]

A further problem with the status anxiety theory is that the graphs Wilkinson and Pickett provide to show evidence of rising anxiety do not correlate with changes in inequality, a point that they explicitly concede when they write that 'We are not suggesting that [these rises in anxiety] were triggered by increased inequality ... the rises in anxiety and depression seem to start well before the increases in inequality which in many countries took place during the last quarter of the twentieth century' (Wilkinson and Pickett 2009: 35). If people have become more anxious since the 1950s, a number of explanations could be given, including Wilkinson and Pickett's own suggestion that it is the result of 'the break-up of the settled communities of the past' (ibid.: 42). This is plausible, but it has nothing to do with inequality and Wilkinson and Pickett ultimately resort to saying that 'Although the rises in anxiety that seem to centre on social evaluation pre-date the rise in inequality it is not difficult to see how rising inequality and social status differences may impact on them' (ibid.). For a book that prides itself on the use of empirical data, this is a weak and speculative claim. In fact, it *is* difficult to see how inequality impacts upon 'the

---

3   Wilkinson and Pickett argue that suicide rates are higher in more equal countries because depressed egalitarians kill themselves while depressed capitalists kill other people. Among the flaws in this extraordinary argument is the fact that suicide rates are not negatively correlated with murder rates.

rise in anxiety' since neither anxiety nor self-esteem move in tandem with inequality.

But even if inequality was linked to anxiety, it is very difficult to see how this could lead to higher rates of infant mortality, lower rates of recycling or higher rates of teen births (to take just three of the outcomes which Wilkinson and Pickett claim are caused by income disparities). Infant mortality in wealthy countries, for example, is largely the result of congenital abnormalities, birth defects, premature births and complications during labour. Most of the babies involved are born critically ill, often with relatively rare medical conditions that are almost entirely unrelated to socioeconomic circumstance. Moreover, some ethnic groups are at greater risk of having premature births (Villadsen et al. 2009), while other ethnic groups are at greater risk of having babies with congenital abnormalities (Balarajan et al. 1989). Even if we believe that income inequality has profound 'psychosocial' effects, the psychological state of the mother has little, if any, bearing on these medical problems. It is likewise very difficult to imagine stress, envy and anxiety having much effect on levels of state aid to foreign countries, participation in recycling, or rates of imprisonment, not least because all are largely dictated by government policy.

Wilkinson and Pickett appear to be on stronger ground when it comes to their key claim about life expectancy since it is well known that stress plays a part in some diseases. They concede that inequality is not linked to many common killers such as breast and prostate cancer, but claim that 'this contrasts sharply with deaths from causes

Figure 17 **Inequality and heart disease mortality (per 100,000)**

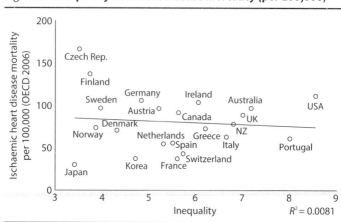

Inequality $R^2 = 0.0081$

such as heart disease which do have a strong social gradient' (Wilkinson and Pickett 2010: 280). If this were true then we should find that less equal countries have higher rates of heart disease, and the correlation between inequality and heart disease should be stronger than the correlation with life expectancy. The authors do not include a graph showing this correlation and, as we can see from Figure 17, no such correlation exists. Indeed, the evidence shows that rates of killer diseases in the West are either inversely related to inequality or not related at all (Mellor and Milyo 2001).

Selective criteria

There is a bias not only in the selection of countries, but also in the criteria that are selected for examination. For example, Wilkinson and Pickett focus on illegal drug use but do not mention alcohol abuse or smoking rates. They devote a chapter to the higher rates of imprisonment in less equal countries without discussing crime rates. They discuss recycling but not unemployment. They show homicide rates but not suicide rates. They look at levels of self-reported trust but not self-reported happiness. They look at teen births but not single parent families. As some of the book's Swedish critics drily concluded: 'It is impressive that the choice of variables used by Wilkinson and Pickett was so precise as to, with no bias in their method, select exactly the combination of countries and measures that suggests there is a statistically significant relationship [between inequality and societal problems]' (Sanandaji et al. 2010: 5–6).

It is a strange index of social problems that excludes key indicators like crime, divorce, unemployment and suicide. In almost every case, the criteria that are excluded either have no association with inequality or are more prevalent in the more equal countries. Wilkinson and Pickett give quite the opposite impression. In the course of their book, they strongly imply – and sometimes explicitly state – that people in egalitarian societies are more philanthropic, suffer fewer family break-ups and are more involved in the local community, but it is actually the people in less equal countries who give more to charity, have fewer divorces and are most likely to be members of community associations.

In a tongue-in-cheek imitation of Wilkinson and Pickett's methods, the sociologist Peter Saunders constructed

Figure 18 **Inequality and per capita cinema attendance**

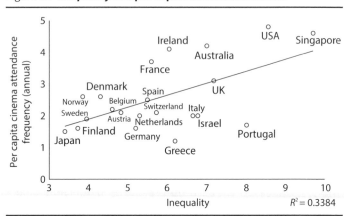

a 'Social Misery Index' comprising suicide, divorce, (lack of) fertility, alcohol consumption, racist bigotry and HIV infection to 'prove' that less equal countries nearly always do better. By his own admission, this index was compiled by 'trawling through the international comparative statistics to find any indicator which varies positively with income inequality' (Saunders 2010: 106). There are so many criteria against which to map inequality – and so many different datasets for each one of them – that correlations abound. Figure 18, for example, shows the statistically significant relationship between income inequality and per capita cinema attendance (UNESCO n.d.). The correlation is at least as strong as most of the graphs in *The Spirit Level* and yet it is extremely difficult to come up with a plausible explanation for why inequality should cause more people

Figure 19 **Inequality and faith in God**

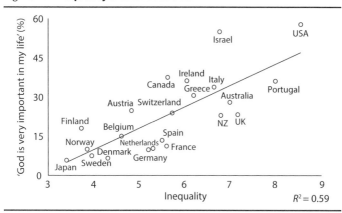

to go to the cinema (or perhaps going to the cinema some-how causes inequality?). Nor is it easy to explain the even stronger correlation between inequality and belief in God shown in Figure 19. I am not, of course, claiming a causal link in either case, but it shows that statistically signifi-cant correlations of the sort that appear in *The Spirit Level* are not hard to find.

Rather than rely on Wilkinson and Pickett's choice of criteria, one way of testing their hypothesis is to apply their method to criteria that have been chosen by inde-pendent others. The Economist Intelligence Unit's 'qual-ity-of-life index' and the OECD's Better Life Index offer a good opportunity to do so. Both indices rank countries according to a range of important criteria, such as health, community, family life, political stability, life sat-isfaction and the environment. When matched against

Figure 20 **Inequality and *The Economist*'s Quality of Life index**

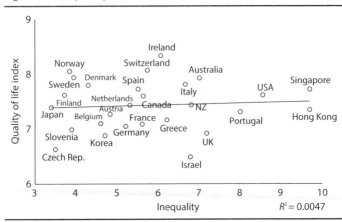

$R^2 = 0.0047$

inequality, neither shows a correlation. In the case of the quality-of-life index (shown in Figure 20), an association with inequality is explicitly ruled out (Economist Intelligence Unit 2005: 3):

> There is no evidence for an explanation sometimes proffered for the apparent paradox of increasing incomes and stagnant life-satisfaction scores: the idea that an increase in someone's income causes envy and reduces the welfare and satisfaction of others. In our estimates, the level of income inequality had no impact on levels of life satisfaction. Life satisfaction is primarily determined by absolute, rather than relative, status (related to states of mind and aspirations).

Consensus?

For over twenty years, Richard Wilkinson has been the leading proponent of the theory that there is a link between income inequality and health, but other researchers have also tested the hypothesis. There have been conflicting results, but a review of 98 studies, published in 2004, concluded that 'The evidence suggests that income inequality is not associated with population health differences – at least not as a general phenomenon – among wealthy nations' (Lynch et al. 2004). This is also the view of the academics who summarised the evidence in the *Oxford Handbook of Economic Inequality* (2009) and concluded that (Leigh et al. 2009):

> the relationship between income inequality and health is either non-existent or too fragile to show up in a robustly estimated panel specification. The best cross-national studies now uniformly fail to find a statistically reliable relationship between economic inequality and longevity ... Our reading of the evidence is that most studies of health and inequality find no statistically significant relationship either across countries or over time.

Other claims made in *The Spirit Level* have not received anywhere near as much attention among researchers as the health-inequality hypothesis. Aside from some of their claims about violent crime, Wilkinson and Pickett's theories are supported mainly, and often exclusively, by studies written by themselves. This was acknowledged by Richard

Wilkinson in 2010 when he told *International Socialism* magazine (Ferguson 2010):

> There are about 200 papers on health and inequality in lots of different settings, probably 40 or 50 looking at violence in relation to inequality, and very few looking at any of the other things in relation to inequality. In a way, the new work in the book is all these other variables – teenage births, mental illness, prison populations and so on – and the major contribution is bringing all of that into a picture that had previously been just health and violence.

For the most part, therefore, these are very much Wilkinson and Pickett's own ideas and their main evidence consists of the kind of scatterplots discussed above. It was only after *The Spirit Level* began to be criticised on empirical grounds that its authors started to insist that a scientific consensus was behind them and that their book was a distilled version of mainstream research (Wilkinson and Pickett (2010b: 1); see Goldthorpe (2009), Kay (2009), Snowdon (2010), Saunders (2010a), Sanandaji et al. (2010) and Bjornskov (2010) for some of the early critical appraisals). In fact, there is no consensus on the inequality-health question and very little research at all behind most of their other claims. In an open letter to Wilkinson and Pickett, the sociologist Colin Mills (2012) wrote: 'Over and over again you tell us that the weight of the evidence is on your side and that there is a broad consensus amongst experts working in the field. But this simply isn't true, is it?' Indeed it is not.

The panacea temptation

The debate about inequality has traditionally been about fairness on the one hand and efficiency on the other. Gross inequalities of wealth[4] and income strike many of us as being unfair, but it is generally understood that there is a trade-off between economic growth and economic equality – if we reduce incentives for people to work and take risks by introducing radical wealth redistribution, the cake will get smaller and everyone will get a little less. A certain amount of inequality is inevitable in a free society and, as an incentive for those who want to get rich, inequality is desirable. Few of us see total income parity as the ideal. Indeed, it would strike many of us as being deeply unfair if hard-working people earned the same as those who work little or never. Nevertheless, it should be clear that the question of what is 'fair' is a moral one that has no objective answer.

The Spirit Level tries to settle this old political question using social science. Wilkinson and Pickett attempt to medicalise the issue of inequality, emphasising the epidemiological comparisons and comparing what they call their 'discovery' with the medical breakthroughs of Joseph Lister and Louis Pasteur (this, of course, was before they started claiming that they were merely distilling a vast body of research by others). There are, I think,

---

4 Wilkinson and Pickett look at income inequality rather than wealth inequality, but the two measures produce markedly different results. Household wealth is distributed more equally in the UK than in France, Sweden and Denmark (Davies et al. 2008).

three reasons for this medicalisation. Firstly, they want to portray income inequality as a disease, because modern societies wage war on diseases and try to wipe them out. Secondly, they want to equate the social sciences with the physical sciences, as if their method of compiling graphs from aggregate data was on a par with laboratory experiments and randomised control trials. Thirdly, by presenting their work as hard science rather than sociology, they are able to present themselves as non-ideological, as if two people in lab coats had taken a politically sensitive topic and looked at it dispassionately.

But none of this stands up. The soft social sciences are always going to provide more equivocal evidence than the physical sciences. Within the field of epidemiology, 'ecological studies' – in which aggregate data from whole societies are compared – are well-known to be the least reliable and the most open to interpretation. 'The epidemiology comparison is artful', writes Charles Moore, 'because it makes the reader believe we can stop inequality just as we stopped smallpox. But of course we cannot. This is a political tract, and, underneath the graphs and the health-talk, a surprisingly traditional socialist one' (Moore 2010).

The fact is that the political debate between right and left is not going to be resolved by social science. It is surprising that anyone ever thought it could. We have to remind ourselves just what a sweeping theory is being presented in *The Spirit Level*. We are being told that our psychological response to a single economic variable is the major predictor and cause of a huge range of highly complex health and social problems. By the same token, if we adjust that single economic variable we can radically improve the performance of a whole country in dozens of totally different ways. Wilkinson and Pickett are offering society a panacea and, like all panaceas, it is too good to be true.

As intuitive as some people found the hypothesis, we also know intuitively that there is no 'theory of everything', as *The Guardian* described *The Spirit Level*'s hypothesis upon publication (Crace 2009). It is supremely unlikely that 'almost every social problem common in developed societies – reduced life expectancy, child mortality, drugs, crime, homicide rates, mental illness and obesity – has a single root cause' (ibid.). And yet a monocausal explanation for virtually everything from infant mortality to recycling was so appealing that the unlikelihood of such a grand unifying theory suddenly being unearthed by two social scientists led people who should know better to allow their credulity to get the better of them.

Why inequality?

There is no doubt that poverty is linked to many of the problems discussed in *The Spirit Level*, including obesity, teen pregnancies, crime and poor health. Nor is there any doubt that there is a socioeconomic gradient for many health and social problems. Life expectancy and educational achievement tend to be lowest among the poor and improve incrementally higher up the income ladder. Similarly, rates of infant mortality, cot death, teen pregnancies and obesity are incrementally lower on each step up the income ladder.

Inequality and poverty are often conflated in the public's mind and so it is important to remember that Wilkinson and Pickett are not writing about poverty, only inequality. Their argument is not merely that the poor suffer the worst outcomes, but that outcomes worsen throughout society because of the psychological damage that is supposedly wrought by inequality. Free-market economists understand that there is a socioeconomic gradient for many health and social problems, but believe that the solution is to make everybody wealthier through economic growth. Wilkinson and Pickett explicitly challenge this view, stating that wealthy societies today are rich enough and that it is now the gap that counts, not wealth per se. They believe that inequality is not merely an economic indicator, but a direct cause of outcomes.

Why not simply write a book about the negative effects of poverty? Perhaps the answer lies in the authors' politics and the politics of a section of the post-Soviet left. Far from being a politically impartial scholar of inequality, Richard Wilkinson is a long-standing campaigner for left-wing causes and a prominent member of the Socialist Health Association. He and Pickett are the founders of two political pressure groups, the Equality Trust and the One Society. By the time we reach the closing chapters of *The Spirit Level*, any pretence of political neutrality has gone out of the window and the authors are calling for a slew of socialist policies. We saw in Chapter 7 that socialism's inability to fulfil its original promise of outperforming capitalism as an engine of prosperity led some left-wingers to reject economic growth as a false god while attacking the free market for increasing inequality, damaging the environment and encouraging excessive consumerism. For those who remain committed to government control over the economy (sometimes misleadingly termed 'democratic control'[5]), it is no longer credible to claim that socialism is the most efficacious system of making the poor richer. They can, however, plausibly claim to be able to make incomes more equal, there being nothing difficult about levelling down. This has led to a growing obsession with the gap between incomes, rather than the size of incomes. *The Spirit Level* represents the *reductio ad absurdum* version of this preoccupation with the gap. A book about the ill effects of poverty could not reasonably conclude that socialism is the answer. A book about inequality can.

Conclusion

Some people will argue that whatever the weaknesses of *The Spirit Level* as a piece of research, it can do no harm to bring attention to what they see as the fundamental unfairness of income inequality. There are, however, several reasons why basing policy on *The Spirit Level* would be foolish. Bad science usually makes for bad policy, whatever the original intentions. Wilkinson and Pickett seem

---

5 Democratic control sounds more appealing than state control, but neither gives control to the individual in any meaningful sense. As Seldon (2004: 179) says: 'The machinery of social control has never been devised. There is no conceivable way in which the British citizen can control the controllers of 'his' state railways or NHS, except so indirectly that it is in effect inoperative.'

indifferent to how inequality is reduced and explicitly state that economic growth is not the answer. By their rationale, society would improve if the poor got 5 per cent poorer so long as the rich got 20 per cent poorer. Rounding up Britain's millionaires and sailing them to the Antarctic would therefore not only make life better for the poor but would make life better for everyone. This is highly implausible. We saw in the last chapter that inequality fell during the economic downturn of 2008–12 without bringing any obvious benefits to anyone. Without a compelling reason to believe that a reduction in inequality for its own sake would materially benefit people on low incomes, the authors leave themselves open to accusations of trading in the politics of envy.

Herein lies the problem with focusing on relative income instead of absolute income. There are things we can do to make the poor richer which might also reduce inequality, and vice versa, but the two objectives are not always compatible. Raising the income tax threshold, for example, should make the poor richer, but if the rich find ways to get even richer in the meantime, will the resulting inequality make things worse for the poor? It is not obvious that it would and yet the logic of *The Spirit Level* says that it must.

Finally, we must remember that there are serious issues at stake here. Each of the problems that are said to be caused by inequality in *The Spirit Level* has been studied much more thoroughly by specialists in the field. Experts often have a pretty good understanding of what can be done to improve people's health, what causes crime, and why rates of murder, infant mortality and teen births vary between countries. They do not offer panaceas but they can offer enlightenment. So long as we have a grasp of the real causes of society's problems, we can do something about them, but if politicians are encouraged to devote their energy and resources to adjusting a single economic variable, they will ignore difficult questions in favour of easy answers.

11 IF YOU'RE BORN POOR, YOU DIE POOR

'Sadly, we still live in a country where, invariably, if you're born poor, you die poor' (BBC 2011). These words, spoken by the 'social mobility tsar' Alan Milburn MP in 2011, are unambiguous in asserting that accidents of birth rigidly determine the fate of the British people. They reflect a conventional wisdom that is constantly reinforced by politicians, journalists and pressure groups – that what little social mobility ever existed in the UK is now in decline. Rafael Behr writes of Britain's 'soul-sapping immobility' in the *New Statesman* (Behr 2012). Polly Toynbee tells *Guardian* readers that the British have become 'more hermetically sealed into the social class of their birth' since the 1970s (Toynbee 2011).

During the Blair years, the presumed decline in social mobility – like the alleged rise in inequality – became a stick with which both the Labour left and the Conservative opposition beat the government. The accusation has persisted, with Michael Gove insisting in 2010 that 'social mobility went backwards under Labour' (Shepherd 2010). The political right blames poor parenting and the decline of grammar schools while the left blames institutional prejudice and income inequality. All of this is based on a misunderstanding of the evidence. The truth is that British society is as socially mobile as it has ever been and probably more so.

Absolute and relative mobility

Until quite recently, social mobility research was the domain of sociologists. The consensus opinion in academia was that structural changes to the labour market in the mid-to-late twentieth century greatly expanded the size of the middle class, meaning that the odds of working-class children becoming middle-class adults became significantly shorter. As the working class shrank and the number of white collar jobs rose, a revolution in *absolute mobility* took place. This was great news for millions of upwardly mobile workers, but it was not the whole story. Sociologists also focus on *relative mobility*, which refers to fluidity between the classes. Unlike absolute mobility, relative mobility is a zero-sum game. For one person to move up, another must move down. The academic consensus was that in relative terms, mobility had remained quite constant, or had become slightly more fluid, since the 1960s, but nobody thought that relative mobility had actually got worse.

Starting in 2001, however, the economist Jo Blanden and colleagues published a series of papers looking at inter-generational income mobility using two British cohorts, one born in 1958, the other born in 1970 (Blanden et al. 2001). Parents' income was measured when they (the children) were 16 years old. Their own income was measured when they were in their early thirties. Blanden et al.

came to a surprising conclusion. In the space of just twelve years, they said, there were 'sharp falls in cross-generation mobility of economic status between the cohorts' (ibid.: 13). The researchers hypothesised that this was due to the middle classes capitalising on the expansion of higher education in the second half of the twentieth century. Their finding, they said, 'flatly contradicts the common view that anyone can make it in modern Britain' (Blanden et al. 2002: i). This was hyperbole, but it certainly supported a more pessimistic view of social mobility than had previously been held.

Blanden et al. were subsequently funded and promoted by the Sutton Trust, a think tank which was founded to promote greater social mobility. In the academic debate that followed, new research was brought to the table. Goldthorpe and Jackson (2007) found that relative mobility for both men and women had remained 'essentially constant' in the post-war era, and when Goldthorpe and Mills (2008) studied data from 1972 and 2005, they again found that social mobility had not been declining. Much the same conclusions were drawn by Paterson and Iannelli (2007), Lambert et al. (2007), Li and Devine (2011) and others.

Some researchers found that relative mobility had actually improved somewhat, such as Heath and Payne (2000), who concluded that there had been a 'real, albeit small, increase in the openness of British society.' Likewise, Li and Devine (2011: 9) found a 'weakening association between origin and destination classes over time', with 'increasing social fluidity over the period covered [1991 to 2005] even though the extent of the increase is rather small'. All agreed with John Goldthorpe, who stated unequivocally in his most recent study that 'if intergenerational mobility is considered in terms of social class, then, with relative just as with absolute rates, *there is no evidence at all to support the idea of mobility in decline*' (emphasis in the original) (Bukodi et al. 2014: 17).

What could explain the divergence between Blanden et al.'s findings and the rest? Part of the explanation lies in the fact that sociologists tend to study class, principally measured by occupation, whereas Blanden et al. focus on income. There are pros and cons to each of these methods. Income is easier to quantify, but occupational status is less prone to temporary fluctuations and misreporting.

Both sides in this debate accept their opponent's evidence when taken at face value. Blanden accepts that 'when social class is used as the measure of status there is little change in mobility' (Blanden et al. 2013) while Goldthorpe accepts that Blanden's data do indeed show that income mobility has declined (Erikson and Goldthorpe 2010). And yet their findings appear to be irreconcilable. We would expect greater class mobility to lead to greater income mobility, but if Blanden et al. are correct, this seems not to be the case.

Erikson and Goldthorpe (2010) argue that there are flaws in the income data that render Blanden et al.'s findings unreliable. They argue that 'one-shot measures of current income' are poorer indicators of economic status than class because they are prone to temporary changes in circumstance. Peter Saunders (2010b: 46) has pointed out that the income snapshot for the 1958 cohort was taken during the three-day-week of 1974 when incomes were particularly unstable. It has also been noted that only 13 per cent of the people involved in the income surveys ended up in the analysis of Blanden et al., thus weakening its statistical power (Gorard 2008). As a result of these and other methodological problems, such as excluding the self-employed from the analysis, it has been argued that the 1958 cohort showed an implausibly weak relationship between the earnings of fathers and sons which made the 1970 cohort look relatively less mobile even though there had been no real change.

Meanwhile, new evidence has undermined Blanden's hypothesis that higher education has become increasingly dominated by the middle class (Boliver 2011; Ianelli et al. 2011). In fact, as Goldthorpe notes: 'social class differences in access to higher education, though wide, remained essentially unchanged [in the late twentieth century]' (Goldthorpe 2012: 9). In response, Blanden has argued plausibly that the contrasting findings for class mobility and income mobility are not necessarily incompatible, but can be explained by wider earnings gaps within the seven occupational classes studied by sociologists (Blanden et al. 2013).

There is, then, a legitimate academic debate about why Blanden's findings on income mobility are at odds with the bulk of the social mobility literature. Much of this debate hinges on technical and methodological issues that elude the average pundit and politician, but it should be noted that none of the academics involved claim that movement between *occupational classes* has become less fluid over time. And so, when Polly Toynbee writes that the Blanden studies prove that the British have become 'more hermetically sealed into the social class of their birth' over time, she is simply wrong, as is Dominic Sandbrook when he laments the 'sad death of opportunity in an increasingly class-bound Britain' (Toynbee 2011; Sandbrook 2012b). The academic debate revolves only around whether the *income mobility* data are sound.

Astonishingly, this debate is hardly ever reflected in the mainstream discussion of social mobility. On the few occasions when the controversy is mentioned, the findings of the sociologists are summarily dismissed. For example, in the coalition government's 2011 report on social mobility entitled *Opening Doors, Breaking Barriers*, the government concedes that:

> The evidence on social mobility is complex and sometimes contradictory.

It nevertheless immediately follows this by asserting (HM Government 2011: 15):

> But the broad picture is fairly clear: We currently have relatively low levels of social mobility, both by international standards and compared with the 'baby boomer' generation born in the immediate post-war period.

At least *Opening Doors, Breaking Barriers* acknowledges the existence of an academic debate. By 2013, the Social Mobility and Child Poverty Commission (2013: 34) was flatly asserting that 'we know that the link between parental and child income seems to have strengthened between the generations born in 1958 and 1970, suggesting a decline in mobility.' The citation for this claim was, as ever, one of Blanden's Sutton Trust studies. Nowhere in this 348 page document was there any reference to the work of John Goldthorpe, Geoff Payne, Peter Saunders, Yaojun Li, Fiona Devine, Stephen Gorard, Michelle Jackson or Colin Mills.

The empirical foundation for the two central claims that social mobility in Britain is (a) declining and (b) worse than in other countries[1] comes almost exclusively from the interpretation of a single dataset that spans only a dozen years. In the view of the sociologist Stephen Gorard, 'one study based on a re-analysis of cohort figures appears to have had an impact on policy-makers out of all proportion to its scale and rigour' (Gorard 2008). No wonder John Goldthorpe (2012: 9) can write, with a hint of exasperation, that 'not only does the consensus view of declining mobility in

---

1   It is notoriously difficult to compare rates of social mobility between countries. 'While it is tempting to immediately form the estimates into a "league table"' writes Blanden (2009: 15), 'we must pay attention to the size of the standard errors; these are large in many cases. Although it does seem to be the case that the Nordic nations have higher mobility, it is impossible to statistically distinguish the estimates for Sweden and the US.' Similarly, the OECD says that 'comparing cross-country estimates of intergenerational income mobility requires a great deal of caution' (d'Addio 2007: 29). Richard Wilkinson and Kate Pickett nevertheless compare these estimates in *The Spirit Level* in an effort to prove that social mobility is lower in less equal countries.

Britain rest empirically on a single piece of research, it rests in effect on the interpretation of a single variable, the family income variable, constructed in the course of this research.'

It is, of course, possible that the view of Blanden et al. is correct, but there are plenty of reasons to suspect that it is not, as Goldthorpe (2012: 11) explains:

> Why, then, should this alternative view [that relative mobility has *not* got worse] be preferred to the consensus view? One rather obvious reason is that the alternative view is based on a far greater body of evidence. Instead of resting on the results of just one piece of research comparing the experience of two birth cohorts only twelve years apart (and in which the reliability of the comparison can be queried), the alternative view rests on a whole series of studies using different designs and data sources but covering the experience of men and women within the British population at large from the 1930s through to the 1980s, and producing remarkably consistent findings.

Wherever the truth lies in this academic debate, it is extraordinary that the controversial findings from a single dataset overshadowed a larger body of research and dominated popular thinking about social mobility so completely. In their original 2004 study, Blanden et al. noted that 'many observers seem to think that we now live in a more mobile, meritocratic society than in the past' (Blanden et al. 2002: i). Such has been the impact of their research that few would voice such an opinion today.

Table 1   **Relative mobility in the UK**

Parent's income	Son's income (bottom)	Son's income (second)	Son's income (third)	Son's income (top)
Bottom	0.38	0.25	0.21	0.16
Second	0.29	0.28	0.26	0.17
Third	0.22	0.26	0.28	0.25
Top	0.11	0.22	0.24	0.42

A number of factors were responsible for the pessimistic view of social mobility becoming the conventional wisdom. John Goldthorpe attributes it to the media savvy of the Sutton Trust (Blanden herself has written of the 'quite extraordinary media reaction' to her research (Blanden 2013)), as well as the political opportunism of both the Labour Party, which wished to portray its predecessor's term in office as a time of declining prospects for the poor, and the Conservative Party, which used the narrative of falling social mobility to condemn Labour's supposed failure to turn the tide. Peter Saunders (2012: 29–30) argues that the complexity of the evidence, combined with the inclination of politicians to encourage a culture of despair, and the long-standing portrayal of Britain in film, television and literature as an 'unfair, class-ridden country' also played a part in feeding the narrative. Whatever the reasons, the outcome was, as Goldthorpe (2012: 7) says, that once the Sutton Trust

> [had] successfully got across the idea of declining mobility to the socio-political commentariat, any different view had little chance of serious consideration. Commentators apparently read each other rather than taking note of new research developments.

Towards a meritocracy

Leaving aside the debate about relative income mobility, certain established facts should be emphasised. No serious academic claims that *class mobility* has declined in the past fifty years, nor does anyone deny that Britain experienced a great expansion in absolute mobility which has slowed, but not retreated, in recent years. And, while Jo Blanden stands by her work, she has complained that it has often been misrepresented, writing that it 'is certainly not true that mobility has "ground to a halt" or "fallen to its lowest level"' (Blanden 2013). As for Alan Milburn claiming that 'invariably, if you're born poor, you die poor', he is simply wrong. As we saw in Chapter 5, every generation has been significantly wealthier than the last for two hundred years or more. The poor get richer.

It may be that Milburn was not talking about the poor getting wealthier in absolute terms, but rather about their position relative to others. If so, the relative mobility (fluidity) figures show that he is wrong about this too. Even if we rely only on Blanden et al.'s income data for the 1970 cohort who came of age during the supposed decline in mobility, we see that there is still extensive movement between the classes (see Table 1 – taken from Saunders (2010b: 38)). In a perfectly fluid society, we would expect 25 per cent (0.25) of the people born into any of the four income brackets to stay there, while the other three-quarters would be evenly spread across the other quartiles. The data above show that this is roughly what happens most of the time. There is a great deal of upward and downward fluidity, particularly considering that this dataset shows social mobility at its worst. It is true that movement from the bottom quartile to the top quartile (and vice versa) is less common than movement between the other quartiles, but it is clearly not the case that those who are born poor, invariably die poor. On the contrary, most of the people who were born into the bottom quartile have moved into a higher income bracket by the time they are in their early thirties, including 16 per cent who are in the top quartile. This is not perfect mobility, but it hardly implies 'soul-sapping immobility'.

Perfect mobility between the classes, in which the chance of ending up in the top or bottom quartile is entirely independent of the circumstances of your birth, does not exist anywhere, but Britain may be more meritocratic than we think. In a meritocracy, we would expect intelligent people to earn more. Generally speaking, they do. Peter Saunders's analysis of the evidence leads him to conclude that (Saunders 2010b: 84):

> [I]f you had to bet on which social class a child born in 1958 would end up in, and you could ask for just one item of information to help with your prediction, the information you would want would not be the parents' social class, nor the type of school the child went to, nor even the degree of support and encouragement the child received from its parents as it was growing up. The information you would want would be the child's IQ test result at age 11.

The advantages enjoyed by those born to wealthy parents are not trivial, but intelligence is more important in modern Britain. 'Cognitive ability,' says Saunders, 'is more than twice as important as class origins in influencing occupational outcomes. Half of the explained variance in occupational outcomes at age 33 can be explained by cognitive ability alone' (ibid.: 87).

If intelligence and ability play a major role in how individuals progress in life, this should be welcomed by those who believe in meritocracy. It suggests that bright children from poor families move upwards while less bright children from wealthy families move downwards. Saunders provides evidence that this is exactly what happens a lot of the time and to a much greater extent than many people believe. And yet Goldthorpe dismisses Saunders's view as 'a position that sociologists would be very unlikely to accept' (Goldthorpe 2012: 27). The resistance lies in the fact that intelligence is heritable to a significant extent and so it stands to reason that some children have an inherent advantage in the labour market that goes beyond the privilege of their parents' wealth. 'A conventional summary is that about half of the variation in intelligence, personality, and life outcomes is heritable,' writes Steven Pinker (2003: 374). In a society in which traditional, non-genetic obstacles to mobility, such as overt class discrimination and huge inequalities in education, become less important, genetic factors must become more important. This should not be controversial. It is, says Pinker, merely a 'banal ... mathematical necessity' (ibid.: 107).

If sociologists are 'unlikely to accept' these findings, it is because they cling to a belief that people are born without innate, inherited characteristics, a view that Pinker calls the 'Blank Slate' theory. Many social scientists continue to be dismissive of IQ tests which, they say, are poor measures of cognitive ability.[2] In fact, IQ tests have been shown to be pretty good barometers of intelligence and IQ scores are a good predictor of life outcomes (Schmidt and Hunter 1998). Although faith in the Blank Slate has dwindled since its mid-twentieth-century heyday, buried beneath a mountain of scientific research that shows the importance of inherited and innate characteristics, it survives in certain pockets of academia and offers a bulwark for those who do not want to believe that inequalities of outcome are, to some extent, merited and unavoidable.

The genetic component should not be overstated. Intelligence is only partly heritable and high IQs are widely distributed among different classes. Moreover, intelligence is only one factor that can lead to financial success. It is no substitute for hard work, dedication and luck. Conversely, accidents of birth can create obstacles that may be virtually insurmountable even for those with excellent cognitive ability. But while we should be wary of taking a deterministic position, the advantage of inherited characteristics,

---

2   But not always. Pinker notes that 'People who say that IQ is meaningless will quickly invoke it when the discussion turns to executing a murderer with an IQ of 64, removing lead paint that lowers a child's IQ by five points, or the presidential qualifications of George W. Bush' (Pinker 2003: 139).

as well as inherited wealth, makes perfect social fluidity unlikely.

There is no country in the world where talent and effort explain *all* the variance in incomes, and there are many countries where these characteristics play a very small role in dictating one's life chances. Britain, however, is not one of them. There are greater opportunities for British workers than ever before in absolute terms and, while social mobility is imperfect in relative terms, there remains an enormous amount of movement between different income groups.

Conclusion

According to Saunders (2010b: 22):

> The big story is that occupational mobility has become more common, and that many more people today have the opportunity to achieve a middle class lifestyle than was the case in the past.

He is talking about the revolution in absolute mobility that came about in the twentieth century and which has not yet ended (a further two million high-skilled, white collar jobs are expected to be created in the 2010s (Wilson and Homenidou 2012: x)). Relative mobility, on the other hand, is a zero-sum game in which the flip-side to upward mobility for one person is downward mobility for another. Downward mobility has obvious negative connotations and politicians do not like to talk about it, but we must have more of it if we are to move towards a meritocracy. Li and Devine (2011: 12) note that academic sociologists are 'exasperated that most politicians and media commentators do not acknowledge that a genuine meritocracy involves downward mobility as well as upward mobility on the basis of merit.' John Goldthorpe confirms this (Derbyshire 2013), saying that Tony Blair

> couldn't see that the only way you can have more upward mobility in a relative perspective is if you have more downward mobility at the same time. I remember being in a discussion in the Cabinet Office when Geoff Mulgan was one of Blair's leading advisors. It took a long time to get across to Mulgan the distinction between absolute and relative rates, but in the end he got it. His response was: 'The Prime Minister can't go to the country on the promise of downward mobility!'

The best-case scenario is one in which there is a great deal of fluidity between the classes while earnings in general increase with productivity. That is what happened in the mid to late twentieth century and, if it feels as if social mobility is now slowing down, it is because that extraordinary expansion of white collar work has – inevitably – slowed down. As Philip Collins (2013) writes:

> The structure of the labour market changed markedly during the 20th century. This is the explanation for the apparent stalling of social mobility. It is telling us nothing more profound than that the rapid growth of

professional employment, which began after the Second World War, has slowed down. In 1900, 18 per cent of jobs were classified in the top two social tiers. By the time John Braine wrote *Room at the Top* [in 1957], that had risen to 42 per cent. But the demand for lawyers and accountants is not inexhaustible.

The point that politicians often fail to grasp is that the dramatic transformation of the labour market in the postwar period cannot be repeated. Those who call for 'a second wave of social mobility' (Shackle 2009) seem unaware of the fact that the first wave had little, if anything, to do with improvements in relative mobility or the expansion of higher education. It was due to structural changes in the labour market which are unlikely to happen again. Goldthorpe's view is that future improvements in absolute mobility will continue to be gradual and, insofar as they depend on government action at all, 'will need to be through economic rather than educational policy: that is, through policy aimed at economic growth' (Goldthorpe 2012: 17).

There is no cause for complacency about social mobility in Britain. The weight of evidence indicates that there has been, at most, only a small improvement in fluidity between the classes in recent decades. There is much work to be done to make sure that people are not unduly hindered by accidents of birth, especially if government policy entrenches the position of particular professions and groups in society. There may be few votes in ensuring more downward mobility, but there is an important issue of fairness in allowing people to rise or fall according to their ability and effort.

The important thing is that capable people are rewarded according to their ability and that productivity is allowed to grow so that the vast majority enjoys better wages than their parents. The gloomy picture of Britain's 'soul-sapping immobility' is not supported by the evidence and it is quite wrong to claim that those who are born poor will 'invariably' die poor. On the contrary, the majority of those who are born poor swiftly move up the income ladder, and almost all become wealthier than their parents.

REFERENCES

Adams, N., Carr, J., Collins, J., Johnson, G. and Matejic, P. (2012)
Households below average income. London: Department for
Work and Pensions.

d'Addio, A. C. (2007) Intergenerational transmission of disad-
vantage. Social, Employment and Migration Working Paper
52. Paris: OECD.

Alesina, A., DiTella, R. and MacCulloch, R. (2004) Happiness and
inequality: are Europeans and Americans different? *Journal
of Public Economics* 88(9–10): 2009–2042.

Anderson, H. (2008) Hurrah for the recession. It will do us a
power of good. *The Guardian*, 17 February.

Ariely, D. (2009) *Predictably Irrational*. London: Harper Collins.

Balarajan, R., Soni Raleigh, V. and Bottling, B. (1989) Sudden
infant death syndrome and postneonatal mortality in im-
migrants in England and Wales. *British Medical Journal*
298(6675): 716–20.

Bastiat, F. (1995) [1850] *Selected Essays on Political Economy*.
New York: Foundation for Economic Education.

Bauman, Z. (2005) *Work, Consumerism and the New Poor*. Maid-
enhead: Oxford University Press.

BBC News (2006) Make people happier, says Cameron. 22 May.

BBC (2011) Labour attacks Nick Clegg over social mobility plan.
5 April.

BBC News (2012) Planning rules on extensions to be relaxed 'to boost economy'. 6 September.

Behr, R. (2012) Inching towards consensus on social mobility. *New Statesman* blog, 2 May.

Ben-Ami, D. (2010) *Ferraris for All: In Defence of Economic Progress*. Bristol: The Policy Press.

Binmore, K. (2007) *Economic Man – or Straw Man?* ESRC Centre for Economic Learning and Social Evaluation.

Bjornskov, C. (2010) Book Reviews: *The Spirit Level*: Why greater equality makes societies stronger. *Population and Development Review* 36(2): 395–96.

Blanchflower, D. (2013) This rockonomics world in which we live is unfair and ultimately bad for growth. *The Independent*, 16 June.

Blanden, J. (2009) How much can we learn from international comparisons of intergenerational mobility? CEE DP 111, London: Centre for the Economics of Education.

Blanden, J. (2013) Social mobility matters, and the government can affect the mechanisms which promote it. LSE blogs, 4 November.

Blanden, J., Goodman, A., Gregg, P. and Machin, S. (2001) Changes in intergenerational mobility in Britain. CMPO Working Paper Series No. 01/43, October.

Blanden, J., Goodman, A., Gregg, P. and Machin, S. (2002) Changes in intergenerational mobility in Britain. CEE DP 26, London: Centre for the Economics of Education.

Blanden, J., Gregg, P. and MacMillan, L. (2013) Intergenerational persistence in income and social class: the impact of within-group inequality. *Journal of the Royal Statistical Society* 176(2): 541–63.

Boaz, D. (2011) Competition and cooperation. In *The Morality of Capitalism* (ed. T. Palmer). Ottawa: Jameson Books.

Boliver, V. (2011) Expansion, differentiation, and the persistence of social class inequalities in British higher education. *Higher Education* 61: 229–42.

Bolt, J. and van Zanden, J. L. (2013) The first update of the Maddison Project; re-estimating growth before 1820. Maddison Project Working Paper 4.

Bosch, G. and Lehndorff, S. (2001) Working-time reduction and employment: experiences in Europe and economic recommendations. *Cambridge Journal of Economics* 25: 209–43.

de Botton, A. (2004) *Status Anxiety*. London: Hamish Hamilton.

Box, G. E. P. and Draper, N. R. (1987) *Empirical Model-Building and Response Surfaces*. London: Wiley.

Brickman, P., Coates, D. and Janoff-Bullman, R. (1978) Lottery winners and accident victims: is happiness relative? *Journal of Personal and Social Psychology* 36(8): 917–27.

Bukodi, E., Goldthorpe, J., Walker, L. and Kuha, J. (2014) The mobility problem in Britain: new findings from the analysis of birth cohort data. *British Journal of Sociology*. (Epub ahead of print.)

Bunting, M. (2009) Recession will deepen inequality. *The Guardian*, 12 August.

Butler, E. (2007) *Adam Smith: A Primer*. London: Institute of Economic Affairs.

Butler, P. (2013) Poverty rose by 900,000 in coalition's first year. *The Guardian*, 13 June.

Caplan, B. (2007) *The Myth of the Rational Voter*. Princeton: Princeton University Press.

Carey, J. (2009) *The Spirit Level*: Why more equal societies almost always do better. *Sunday Times*, 8 August.

Carrera, S. and J. Beaumont (2010) Income and wealth. Social Trend 41, Office for National Statistics.

Centers for Disease Control (2012) Birth rates for U.S. teenagers reach historic lows for all age and ethnic groups. NCHS Data Brief. Number 89, April.

Chang, H. (2010) *23 Things They Don't Tell You About Capitalism*. London: Allen Lane.

Chote, R. (1994) Recession narrows the gap between wealthy and poor. *The Independent*, 1 February.

Clark, G. (2007) *A Farewell to Alms: A Brief Economic History of the World*. Princeton University Press.

Collins, P. (2013) The social mobility myth. *Prospect*, October.

Cooper, R. (2011) Pay gap between highest and lowest earners growing faster in Britain than any of the world's richest countries. *Daily Mail*, 5 December.

Cowen, T. (2004) How do economists think about rationality? In *Satisficing and Maximizing – Moral Theorists on Practical Reason* (ed. M. Byron). Cambridge University Press.

Crace, J. (2009) The theory of everything. *The Guardian*, 1 March.

Cribb, J., Joyce, R. and Phillips, D. (2012) *Living Standards, Poverty and Inequality in the UK: 2012*. London: Institute of Fiscal Studies.

Cribb, J. (2013) *Income Inequality in the UK*. London: Institute of Fiscal Studies.

Davies, J. B., Sandstrom, S., Shorrocks, A. and Wolff, E. (2008) The world distribution of household wealth. WIDER Discussion Paper 3.

Deaton, A. (2008) Income, health and wellbeing around the world: evidence from the Gallup World Poll. *Journal of Economic Perspectives* 22(2): 53–72.

Department for Transport (2013) *National Travel Survey.* London: Department for Transport.

Derbyshire, J. (2013) Room at the top. *Prospect*, September.

Dorling, D., Rigby, J., Wheeler, B., Ballas, D., Thomas, B., Fahmy, E., Gordon, D. and Lupton, R. (2007) *Poverty, Wealth and Place in Britain, 1968–2005.* Bristol: The Policy Press.

Drago, R., Wooden, M. and Black, D. (2009) Who wants and gets flexibility? Changing work hours preferences and life events. *IRL Review* 62(3): 394–414.

Easterlin, R. (1974) Does economic growth improve the human lot? Some empirical evidence. In *Nations and Households in Economic Growth: Essays in Honour of Moses Abramowitz* (ed. P. David and M. Reder), pp. 89–125. New York: Academic Press.

Easton, M. (2006) The politics of happiness. BBC, 22 May.

Eckblad, G. and von der Lippe, A. (1994) Norwegian lottery winners: cautious realists. *Journal of Gambling Studies* 10(4): 305–22.

Economist (2011) Unbottled Gini. 20 January.

Economist Intelligence Unit (2005) The Economist Intelligence Unit's quality-of-life index.

Erikson, R. and Goldthorpe, J. (2010) Income and class mobility between generations in Great Britain: the problem of divergent findings from the data-sets of British cohort studies. *British Journal of Sociology* 61(2): 211–30.

European Foundation for the Improvement of Living and Working Conditions (2008) *Revisions to the European Working Time Directive: Recent Eurofund Research.* Dublin.

Faris, S. (2009) A better measure than GDP. *Time*, 2 November.

FBI (2013) Crime in the United States 2012. http://www.fbi.gov

Ferguson, I. (2010) Interview: reviving the spirit of equality. *International Socialism* 127, 24 June.

Flanders, S. (2012) Britain's recession: harsh but fair? BBC website: http://www.bbc.co.uk/news/business-19984877

Friedman, M. (1978) Which way for capitalism? *Reason*, May.

Friedman, M. (2002) *Capitalism and Freedom*. University of Chicago Press.

Friedman, M. and Friedman, R. (1980) *Free to Choose*. New York: Harcourt, Brace and Jovanovich.

Frank, R. (1999) *Luxury Fever*. New York: The Free Press

Galbraith, J. K. (1987) *The Affluent Society*. London: Penguin.

Gardner, D. (2011) Might as well face it, we're addicted to growth. Centre for the Advancement of the Steady State Economy, http://steadystate.org/might-as-well-face-it-were-addicted-to-growth/

Garroway, C. and de Laiglesia, J. (2012) On the relevance of relative poverty for developing countries. OECD Development Centre, Working Paper 314, Paris.

Gillan, A. (2005) Work until you drop: how the long-hours culture is killing us. *The Guardian*, 20 August.

Gleeson-White, J. (2012) Is the reign of GDP as the only measure of wealth coming to an end? *The Guardian*, 22 October.

Goldthorpe, J. (2009) Analysing social inequality: a critique of two recent contributions from economics and epidemiology. *European Sociological Review* 26(6): 731–44.

Goldthorpe, J. (2012) Understanding – and misunderstanding – social mobility in Britain: The entry of the economists, the confusion of politicians and the limits of educational policy. Barnet Papers in Social Research, Department of Social Policy and Intervention, Oxford.

Goldthorpe, J. and Jackson, M. (2007) Intergenerational class mobility in contemporary Britain: political concerns and empirical findings. *British Journal of Sociology* 58(4): 525–46.

Goldthorpe, J. and Mills, C. (2008) Trends in intergenerational class mobility in modern Britain: evidence from national surveys, 1972–2005. *National Institute Economic Review* 205(1): 83–100.

Gorard, S. (2008) A reconsideration of rates of social mobility in Britain: or why research impact is not always a good thing. *British Journal of Sociology of Education* 29(3): 317–24.

Green Party of New Zealand (n.d.) The history of the Green Party. https://home.greens.org.nz/history-green-party

Hamilton, C. and Mail, E. (2003) Downshifting in Australia: a sea-change in the pursuit of happiness. Discussion Paper Number 50, The Australia Institute.

Hargreaves, D. (2013) Inequality is tearing apart our society. *Huffington Post*, 9 October.

Harris, R. and Seldon, A. (1959) *Advertising in a Free Society*. London: Institute of Economic Affairs.

Harwood Group (1995) *Yearning for Balance: Views of Americans on Consumption, Materialism, and the Environment*. Takoma Park, MD: Merck Family Fund.

Hatherley, O. (2012) It's the 21st century – why are we working so much? *The Guardian*, 1 July 2012.

Hayek, F. (1991) *The Trend of Economic Thinking*. London: Routledge.

Hayek, F. (2001) *The Road to Serfdom*. London: Routledge.

Heald, G. and Wybrow, G. (1986). *The Gallup Survey of Britain*. Beckenham: Croom Helm.

Heath, A. and Payne, C. (2000) Social mobility. In *Twentieth-Century British Social Trends* (ed. A. H. Halsey with J. Webb), pp. 254–78. Basingstoke: Macmillan.

Herfeld, C. (2012) The potentials and limitations of rational choice theory: an interview with Gary Becker. *Erasmus Journal for Philosophy and Economics* 5(1): 73–86.

Hertz, N. (2002) *The Silent Takeover*. London: Arrow Books.

Hicks, J. and Allen, G. (1999) A century of change: trends in UK statistics since 1900. House of Commons Library Research Paper 99/111, 21 December.

HM Government (2011) *Opening Doors, Breaking Barriers: A Strategy for Social Mobility*. London: Deputy Prime Minister's Office.

Hutton, W. (2013) Osborne wants to take us back to 1948. Time to look forward instead. *The Guardian*, 8 December.

Ianelli, C., Gamoran, A. and Paterson, L. (2011) Scottish higher education, 1987–2001: expansion through diversion. *Oxford Review of Education* 37: 717–41.

IFS (Institute for Fiscal Studies) (2014) Public spending figures. IFS spreadsheet also available at www.cemmap.ac.uk/uploads/publications/ff/lr_spending.xls

Ipsos MORI (2013) *Understanding Society – Great Britain: The Way We Live Now*. London: Ipsos MORI.

James, O. (2007) *Affluenza*. London: Vermillion.

James, O. (2008) *The Selfish Capitalist*. London: Vermillion.

Japan Times (2002) Investors agree to settle Kobe Steel suit. 6 April.

Japan Times (2006) Kobe Steel punishes execs in smog coverup. 23 June.

Jefferson, T. (2001) *The Inaugural Addresses of President Thomas Jefferson*. Columbia: University of Missouri Press.

Johnson, R. (2012) What about the questions that economics can't answer? *The Exchange* (Yahoo Finance), 24 September.

Jolly, D. (2009) GDP seen as inadequate measure of economic health. *New York Times*, 14 September.

Jones, F., Annan, D. and Shah, S. (2008) The distribution of household income 1977 to 2006/07. *Economic & Labour Market Review* 2(12).

Kahneman, D. and Krueger, A. (2006) Developments in the measurement of subjective well-being. *Journal of Economic Perspectives* 20(1): 3–24.

Kasparova, D., Wyatt, N., Mills, T. and Roberts, S. (2010) *Pay: Who Were the Winners and Losers of the New Labour Era?* London: The Work Foundation.

Kaufman, C. (2012) *Getting Past Capitalism: History, Vision, Hope*. Plymouth: Lexington Books.

Kay, J. (2009) *The Spirit Level. Financial Times*, 23 March.

Kennedy, R. (1968) Address to University of Kansas, Lawrence. Kansas, 18 March.

Keynes, J. M. (2009) *Essays in Persuasion*. New York: Classic House Books.

King, M. (2011) Wage inequality rises across the UK. *The Guardian*, 7 November.

Klein, N. (2000) *No Logo*. New York: Picador.

Kuhn, P. and Lozano, F. (2005) The expanding workweek? Understanding trends in long work hours amongst U.S. men 1979–2004. NBER Working Paper 11895, December 2005.

Kuhn, P., Kooreman, P., Soetevent, A. and Kapteyn, A. (2008) The own and social effects of an unexpected income shock: evidence from the Dutch postcode lottery. RAND Working Paper WR-574.

Kuziemko, I., Norton, M., Saez, E. and Stantcheva, S. (2013) How elastic are preferences for redistribution? Evidence from randomized survey experiments. National Bureau of Economic Research, Working Paper 18865.

Lacey, S. (2012) Measuring human and environmental progress: world leaders call for a new metrics at Rio. Climate Progress, 20 June. http://thinkprogress.org/climate/2012/06/20/502961/measuring-human-and-environmental-progress-world-leaders-call-for-new-metrics-at-rio20/#

Lambert, P., Prandy, K. and Bottero, W. (2008) By slow degrees: two centuries of social reproduction and mobility in Britain. *Sociological Research Online* 13(1).

Lansley, S. (2009) *Unfair to Middling: How Middle Income Britain's Shrinking Wages Fuelled the Crash and Threaten Recovery*. London: Touchstone Extras.

Latouche, S. (2009) *Farewell to Growth*. Cambridge: Polity Press.

Lawson, N. (2009) *All Consuming*. London: Penguin.

Layard, R. (2006) *Happiness: Lessons from a New Science*. London: Penguin.

Lee, N., Sissons, P. and Jones, K. (2013) *Wage Inequality and Employment Polarisation in British Cities*. London: The Work Foundation.

Leigh, A., Jencks, C. and Smeeding, T. M. (2009) Health and economic inequality. In *The Oxford Handbook of Economic Inequality* (ed. W. Salverda, B. Nolvan and T. M. Smeeding), pp. 384–405. Oxford University Press.

Li, Y. and Devine, F. (2011) Is social mobility really declining? Intergenerational class mobility in Britain in the 1990s and the 2000s. *Sociological Research Online* 16(3).

Lynch, J., Due, P., Muntaner, C. and Davey Smith, G. (2000) Social capital – is it a good investment strategy for public health? *Journal of Epidemiology and Community Health* 54: 404–8.

Lynch, J., Smith, G. D., Harper, S., Hillemeier, M., Ross, N., Kaplan, G. and Wolfson, M. (2004) Is income inequality a determinant of population health? Part 1: A systematic review. *Millbank Quarterly* 82(1): 5–99.

Mackenbach, J. (2002) Income inequality and population health. *British Medical Journal* 324(7343): 1–2.

Maddison, A. (2008) The West and the rest in the world economy: 1000–2030. *World Economics* 9(4).

Marx, K. and Engels, F. (2002) *The Communist Manifesto*. London: Penguin.

Meacher, M. (2013) One way to tackle colossal, growing pay inequality. *The Guardian,* 10 October.

Meadowcroft, J. (ed.) (2008) *Prohibitions*. London: Institute of Economic Affairs.

Meadway, J. (2012) No return to boom. New Economics Foundation blog: http://www.neweconomics.org/blog/entry/no-retu rn-to-boom

Mellor, J. and Milyo, J. (2001) Reexamining the evidence of an ecological association between income inequality and health. *Journal of Health Politics, Policy and Law* 26(3): 487–522.

Merrick, J. (2013) Government's welfare benefits and tax changes amount to 'speeded-up Thatcherism'. *The Independent,* 21 July.

Mills, C. (2012) Open letter to Prof. Richard Wilkinson and Prof. Kate Pickett. Oxford Sociologist (blog), 5 November. http://

oxfordsociology.blogspot.co.uk/2012/11/open-letter-to-prof
-richard-wilkinson.html

Minogue, K. (1989) *The Egalitarian Conceit*. London: Centre for Policy Studies.

Monbiot, G. (2013) So you need that smart cuckoo clock for Christmas, do you? *The Guardian,* 25 November.

Moore, C. (2010) Inequality is not a social illness to be 'cured'. *Daily Telegraph*, 9 February.

Moore, S. (2012) Why do we take economists so seriously? *The Guardian,* 6 June.

Morgan, M. (1996) The character of 'rational economic man'. Working Papers in Economic History 34. London School of Economics.

Murphy, R. (2011) *The Courageous State*. London: Searching Finance.

Nasar, S. (2012) *The Grand Pursuit*. London: Fourth Estate.

Nelson, J. (2010) 12 steps to treat our growth addiction. Post Growth:http://postgrowth.org/12-steps-to-treat-our-growth -addiction

NEF (New Economics Foundation) (2004) *Chasing Progress*. London: New Economics Foundation.

NEF (New Economics Foundation) (2010) Economic growth no longer possible for rich countries, says new research. http:// www.neweconomics.org/press/entry/economic-growth-no -longer-possible-for-rich-countries-says-new-research

Norberg, J. (2003) *In Defense of Global Capitalism*. Washington, DC: Cato Institute.

Nordhaus, W. and Tobin, J. (1972) *Is Growth Obsolete? Economic Research: Retrospect and Prospect*, Vol. 5. *Economic Growth*. New York: National Bureau of Economic Research.

Nozick, R. (1974) *Anarchy, State and Utopia*. New York: Basic Books.

O'Neill, D. (2013) The economics of enough. *The Guardian*, 1 May.

O'Rourke, P. J. (2007) *On the Wealth of Nations*. London: Atlantic Books.

OECD (1998) *Employment Outlook*. Paris: OECD.

OECD (2011) *Divided We Stand: Why Inequality Keeps Rising*. Paris: OECD Publishing.

OECD (2012a) Better life index: work-life balance. http://www.oecdbetterlifeindex.org/topics/work-life-balance/

OECD (2012b) Incidence of employment by usual weekly hours worked. http://stats.oecd.org

OECD (2013a) Incidence of involuntary part time workers. http://stats.oecd.org/Index.aspx?DatasetCode=INVPT_I

OECD (2013b) Average annual hours actually worked per worker (2012). http://stats.oecd.org

ONS (Office for National Statistics) (2008) The distribution of household income 1977 to 2006.

ONS (2011a) Hours worked in the labour market – 2011.

ONS (2011b) Commuting to work, 2011. 2 June.

ONS (2012a) Measuring national well-being – the economy. 23 October.

ONS (2012b) Average equivalised household income by quintile group in 2006/07 prices (source data).

ONS (2012c) Real wages up 62% on average over the past 25 years (source data). 7 November.

ONS (2012d) Inequalities and poverty in retirement, 2012 edition. In *Pension Trends*, Chapter 13. 24 October.

ONS (2013a) Middle income households, 1977–2011/12. 2 December.

ONS (2013b) The effects of taxes and benefits on household income, 2011/12. 10 July.

ONS (2013c) The effects of taxes and benefits on household income, 2011/12 (source data).

ONS (2014a) The effects of taxes and benefits on household income, 2012/13. 26 June.

ONS (2014b) UK wages over the past four decades, 2014. 3 July.

Oswald, A. and Powdthavee, N. (2006) Does happiness adapt? A longitudinal study of disability with implications for economists and judges. IZA Discussion Paper 2208.

Oulton, N. (2012) Hooray for GDP! Centre for Economic Performance, London School of Economics and Political Science.

Oxfam GB (2012) Why the Robin Hood tax matters for UK poverty. http://robinhoodtax.org.uk/latest/why-robin-hood-tax -matters-uk-poverty

Pahl, R., Rose, D. and Spencer, L. (2007) Inequality and quiescence: a continuing conundrum. Institute for Social and Economic Research, ISER Working Paper 2007–22.

Palmer, T. (2011) Adam Smith and the myth of greed. In *The Morality of Capitalism* (ed. T. Palmer). Ottawa: Jameson Books.

Parkin, D., Appleby, J. and Maynard, A. (2013) Economics: the biggest fraud ever perpetuated on the world? *The Lancet* 382(9900): e11-e15.

Paterson, L. and Iannelli, C. (2007) Patterns of absolute and relative social mobility: a comparative study of England, Wales and Scotland. *Sociological Research Online* 12(6).

Peck, J. (2012) Is George Osborne questioning capitalism? New Economics Foundation (blog), 9 April.

Pessoa, J. and Van Reenen, J. (2013) Wage growth and productivity growth: the myth and reality of 'decoupling'. CentrePiece, Autumn.

Piketty, T. and Saez, E. (2012) Top incomes and the Great Recession: Recent evolutions and policy implications. 13th Jacques Polak Annual Research Conference.

Pinker, S. (2003) *The Blank Slate: The Modern Denial of Human Nature*. London: Penguin.

Plumer, B. (2012) Mega millions frenzy: can you ever beat the lottery's long odds? *Washington Post* (blogs), 30 March.

Posner, R. (1998) Rational choice, behavioral economics, and the law. *Stanford Law Review* 50: 1551–75.

Prowse, M. (1998) Paternalist government is out of date. In *The Libertarian Reader* (ed. D. Boaz). New York: The Free Press.

Quiggin, J. (2010) *Zombie Economics*. Princeton University Press.

Ramesh, R. (2011) Income inequality growing faster in UK than any other rich country, says OECD. *The Guardian*, 5 December.

Rank, M. R. (2014) From rags to riches to rags. *New York Times*, 18 April.

Reeves, R. (2013) Why RSA's Matthew Taylor has got it wrong (1/2): Income inequality. CentreForum Blog, 6 March: http://centreforumblog.wordpress.com/2013/03/06/richard-reeves-why-rsas-matthew-taylor-has-got-it-wrong-12-income-inequality/

Revel, J.-F. (1977) *The Totalitarian Temptation*. Harmondsworth: Penguin.

Revel, J.-F. (2009) *Last Exit to Utopia: The Survival of Socialism in a Post-Soviet Era*. New York: Encounter Books.

Russell, J. (2010) It's money that matters. *Boston Globe*, 21 February.

Sala-i-Martin, X. (2006) The world distribution of income: falling poverty and ... convergence, period. *Quarterly Journal of Economics* 121(2): 351–97.

Samuel, H. (2009) Nicolas Sarkozy wants to measure economic success in 'happiness'. *Daily Telegraph*, 14 September.

Sanandaji, N., Malm, A. and Sanandaji, T. (2010) *The Spirit Illusion: A Critical Analysis of How 'The Spirit Level' Compares Countries*. London: Taxpayers Alliance.

Sandbrook, D. (2011) *State of Emergency*. London: Allen Lane.

Sandbrook, D. (2012a) *Seasons in the Sun: The Battle for Britain 1974–1979*. London: Allen Lane.

Sandbrook, D. (2012b) How a complacent elite and years of school failure have dimmed the bright lights of opportunity. *Daily Mail*, 2 May.

Saunders, P. (2010a) *Beware False Prophets: Equality, the Good Society and The Spirit Level*. London: Policy Exchange.

Saunders, P. (2010b) *Social Mobility Myths*. London: Civitas.

Saunders, P. (2012) *Social Mobility Delusions*. London: Civitas.

Savage, M., Lea, R. and Costello, M. (2012) Small firms' red tape cut as unions turn militant. *The Times*, 10 September.

Schmidt, F. and Hunter J. (1998) The validity and utility of selection methods in personnel psychology: practical and theoretical implications of 85 years of research findings. *Psychological Bulletin* 124(2): 262–74.

Seldon, A. (2004) *The Collected Works of Arthur Seldon*. Indianapolis: Liberty Fund.

Sen, A. (1977) Rational fools: a critique of the behavioral foundations of economic theory. *Philosophy & Public Affairs* 6(4), Summer: 317–44.

Shackle, S. (2009) Cheat sheet: social mobility. *New Statesman*, 21 July.

Shepherd, J. (2010) Challenge to Gove claim that 'social mobility went backwards under Labour'. *The Guardian*, 27 December.

Simms, A. (2009) 94 months and counting. *The Guardian*, 2 February.

Simon, E. (2013) Rich are 'hardest hit by recession'. *Daily Telegraph*, 4 June.

Simon, H. A. (1955) A behavioral model of rational choice. *Quarterly Journal of Economics* 69(1): 99–118.

Skidelsky, R. (2009) How much is enough? Project Syndicate November 19: http://www.project-syndicate.org/commentary/how-much-is-enough

Skidelsky, R. and Skidelsky, E. (2012a) *How Much Is Enough?* London: Penguin.

Skidelsky, R. and Skidlesky, E. (2012b) In praise of leisure. *Chronicle of Higher Education*, June 18.

Smith, A. (1761) *The Theory of Moral Sentiments*.

Smith, A. (1957) [1776] *An Inquiry into the Nature and Causes of the Wealth of Nations*, Vol. 1. London: J. M. Dunt and Sons.

Smith, A. (1999) *The Wealth of Nations*, Books IV–V. London: Penguin.

Smith, D., Langa, K., Kabeto, M. and Ubel, P. (2005) Health, wealth, and happiness. *Psychological Science* 16(9): 663–66.

Smith, D. (2012) No sir – a 75% tax rate won't hurt. *Sunday Times*, 1 July.

Smith, R. (2011) Beneath the skin: statistics, trust, and status. *Educational Theory* 61(6): 633–45.

Snowdon, C. (2010) *The Spirit Level Delusion*. Ripon: Little Dice.

Snowdon, C. (2012) Are more equal countries happier? In ... *and the Pursuit of Happiness* (ed. P. Booth). London: Institute of Economic Affairs.

Social Mobility and Child Poverty Commission (2013) *State of the Nation 2013: Social Mobility and Child Poverty in Great Britain*. London: Stationery Office.

Sowell, T. (2011) *Intellectuals and Society*. New York: Basic Books.

Stevenson, B. and Wolfers, J. (2008) Economic growth and subjective well-being: reassessing the Easterlin Paradox. NBER Working Paper 14282.

Taleb, N. (2007) *The Black Swan*. London: Penguin.

Thompson, D. (2012) The economic case against winning a $500 million lottery (seriously). *The Atlantic*, 29 November.

Toynbee, P. (2011) Money busts the convenient myth that social class is dead. *The Guardian,* 29 August.

Toynbee, P. (2012) London 2012: Danny Boyle's opening ceremony is only a partial truth. *The Guardian,* 30 July.

UNESCO Institute for Statistics (n.d.) Cinema statistics (Table 12): http://www.uis.unesco.org/CULTURE/Pages/movie-statistics.aspx

United Nations (2013) *Human Development Report 2013*. New York: UN.

Veenhoven, R. and Vergunst, F. (2013) The Easterlin illusion: economic growth does go with greater happiness. Erasmus Happiness Economics Research Organization, Working Paper 2013/1, 23 January.

Villadsen, S., Mortensen, L. and Anderson, A. (2009) Ethnic disparity in stillbirth and infant mortality in Denmark 1981–2003. *Journal of Epidemiology and Community Health* 63(2): 106–12.

Whyte, J. (2013) *Quack Policy*. London: Institute of Economic Affairs.

Wilkinson, R. and Pickett, K. (2009) *The Spirit Level: Why More Equal Societies Almost Always Do Better*. London: Allen Lane.

Wilkinson, R. and Pickett, K. (2010a) *The Spirit Level: Why Equality Is Better for Everyone* (2nd edn). London: Penguin.

Wilkinson, R. and Pickett, K. (2010b) Professors Richard Wilkinson and Kate Pickett, authors of *The Spirit Level*, reply to critics. equalitytrust.org.uk

Williams, Z. (2012) On capitalism we lefties are clueless – it's not just a rightwing caricature. *The Guardian,* 29 February.

Wilson, R. A. and Homenidou, K. (2012) Working Futures 2010–2020. UK Commission for Employment and Skills, Evidence Report 41.

Zilibotti, F. (2007) 'Economic possibilities for our grandchildren' 75 years after: a global perspective. Institute for Empirical Research in Economics, Working Paper 344, December.

ABOUT THE IEA

The Institute is a research and educational charity (No. CC 235 351), limited by guarantee. Its mission is to improve understanding of the fundamental institutions of a free society by analysing and expounding the role of markets in solving economic and social problems.

The IEA achieves its mission by:

- a high-quality publishing programme
- conferences, seminars, lectures and other events
- outreach to school and college students
- brokering media introductions and appearances

The IEA, which was established in 1955 by the late Sir Antony Fisher, is an educational charity, not a political organisation. It is independent of any political party or group and does not carry on activities intended to affect support for any political party or candidate in any election or referendum, or at any other time. It is financed by sales of publications, conference fees and voluntary donations.

In addition to its main series of publications the IEA also publishes a quarterly journal, *Economic Affairs*.

The IEA is aided in its work by a distinguished international Academic Advisory Council and an eminent panel of Honorary Fellows. Together with other academics, they review prospective IEA publications, their comments being passed on anonymously to authors. All IEA papers are therefore subject to the same rigorous independent refereeing process as used by leading academic journals.

IEA publications enjoy widespread classroom use and course adoptions in schools and universities. They are also sold throughout the world and often translated/reprinted.

Since 1974 the IEA has helped to create a worldwide network of 100 similar institutions in over 70 countries. They are all independent but share the IEA's mission.

Views expressed in the IEA's publications are those of the authors, not those of the Institute (which has no corporate view), its Managing Trustees, Academic Advisory Council members or senior staff.

Members of the Institute's Academic Advisory Council, Honorary Fellows, Trustees and Staff are listed on the following page.

The Institute gratefully acknowledges financial support for its publications programme and other work from a generous benefaction by the late Professor Ronald Coase.

Other papers recently published by the IEA include:

Hayek's The Constitution of Liberty – An Account of Its Argument
Eugene F. Miller
Occasional Paper 144; ISBN 978-0-255-36637-3; £12.50

Fair Trade Without the Froth – A Dispassionate Economic Analysis of 'Fair Trade'
Sushil Mohan
Hobart Paper 170; ISBN 978-0-255-36645-8; £10.00

A New Understanding of Poverty – Poverty Measurement and Policy Implications
Kristian Niemietz
Research Monograph 65; ISBN 978-0-255-36638-0; £12.50

The Challenge of Immigration – A Radical Solution
Gary S. Becker
Occasional Paper 145; ISBN 978-0-255-36613-7; £7.50

Sharper Axes, Lower Taxes – Big Steps to a Smaller State
Edited by Philip Booth
Hobart Paperback 38; ISBN 978-0-255-36648-9; £12.50

Self-employment, Small Firms and Enterprise
Peter Urwin
Research Monograph 66; ISBN 978-0-255-36610-6; £12.50

Crises of Governments – The Ongoing Global Financial Crisis and Recession
Robert Barro
Occasional Paper 146; ISBN 978-0-255-36657-1; £7.50

… and the Pursuit of Happiness – Wellbeing and the Role of Government
Edited by Philip Booth
Readings 64; ISBN 978-0-255-36656-4; £12.50

Public Choice – A Primer
Eamonn Butler
Occasional Paper 147; ISBN 978-0-255-36650-2; £10.00

The Profit Motive in Education – Continuing the Revolution
Edited by James B. Stanfield
Readings 65; ISBN 978-0-255-36646-5; £12.50

Which Road Ahead – Government or Market?
Oliver Knipping & Richard Wellings
Hobart Paper 171; ISBN 978-0-255-36619-9; £10.00

Other IEA publications

Comprehensive information on other publications and the wider work of the IEA can be found at www.iea.org.uk. To order any publication please see below.

Personal customers

Orders from personal customers should be directed to the IEA:

Clare Rusbridge
IEA
2 Lord North Street
FREEPOST LON10168
London SW1P 3YZ
Tel: 020 7799 8907. Fax: 020 7799 2137
Email: sales@iea.org.uk

Trade customers

All orders from the book trade should be directed to the IEA's distributor:

NBN International (IEA Orders)
Orders Dept.
NBN International
10 Thornbury Road
Plymouth PL6 7PP
Tel: 01752 202301, Fax: 01752 202333
Email: orders@nbninternational.com

IEA subscriptions

The IEA also offers a subscription service to its publications. For a single annual payment (currently £42.00 in the UK), subscribers receive every monograph the IEA publishes. For more information please contact:

Clare Rusbridge
Subscriptions
IEA
2 Lord North Street
FREEPOST LON10168
London SW1P 3YZ
Tel: 020 7799 8907, Fax: 020 7799 2137
Email: crusbridge@iea.org.uk